Who Am I?

Discovering Our True Identity in Christ
Living the Life Christ Intended Us to Have

ZANTHIA BERKELMANN

WESTBOW
PRESS®
A DIVISION OF THOMAS NELSON
& ZONDERVAN

Scripture quotations are taken from the Holy Bible, New Living Translation,
copyright ©1996, 2004, 2007 by Tyndale House Foundation. Used by permission
of Tyndale House Publishers, Inc., Carol Stream, Illinois 60188. All rights reserved

Scripture taken from the New King James Version®. Copyright ©
1982 by Thomas Nelson. Used by permission. All rights reserved.

THE HOLY BIBLE, NEW INTERNATIONAL VERSION®,
NIV® Copyright © 1973, 1978, 1984, 2011 by Biblica, Inc.®
Used by permission. All rights reserved worldwide.

WestBow Press books may be ordered through booksellers or by contacting:

WestBow Press
A Division of Thomas Nelson & Zondervan
1663 Liberty Drive
Bloomington, IN 47403
www.westbowpress.com
1 (866) 928-1240

Because of the dynamic nature of the Internet, any web addresses or
links contained in this book may have changed since publication and
may no longer be valid. The views expressed in this work are solely those
of the author and do not necessarily reflect the views of the publisher,
and the publisher hereby disclaims any responsibility for them.

Any people depicted in stock imagery provided by Thinkstock are models,
and such images are being used for illustrative purposes only.
Certain stock imagery © Thinkstock.

ISBN: 978-1-5127-6751-3 (sc)
ISBN: 978-1-5127-6752-0 (hc)
ISBN: 978-1-5127-6750-6 (e)

Library of Congress Control Number: 2016920499

Print information available on the last page.

WestBow Press rev. date: 12/10/2016

Table of Contents

Table of Contents

Dedication

To my Lord and Savior, Jesus Christ, to whom I am daily thankful for all he has done in my life and still doing. All praise and honor to him.

Foreword

With this book, I want to share with you my journey to discovering my true identity in Christ and living it to the full every day in every way. I pray you will find nuggets that will transform your life or shine some light on your journey of faith.

Part 1

Chapter 1

Who Am I?

Who am I? I am Zanthia Berkelmann. I am loved, accepted, chosen, and forgiven by God. I am a new creation. I have been made righteous and a member of the royal priesthood, God's special possession.

I am always struck by Jesus's character when I read the Gospels. He knew who he was and what his assignment was. I sensed he felt an urgency in the way he went about some of his ministry and the call on his life. He was secure and confident in his identity as the Son of God. He was intense in everything he undertook. He displayed a discipline like no other in the time he spent with his Father, getting into the Word, teaching the disciples, and going about his ministry. He demonstrated to us the pattern of authentic relationship between God and people. Even though he knew who he was, he was very much dependent on the Father, who had sent him. In John 5:19, Jesus said, "I tell you the truth, the Son can do nothing by himself. He does only what he sees the Father doing. Whatever the Father does, the Son also does."

Through my understanding of Jesus's life and teaching, I am inspired to know who I am in Christ Jesus, grow in that identity, and become more like Jesus.

God so beautifully orchestrated my life so I could become his special possession. I am the apple of his eye, and he adores me! He personally chose me. I did not find him; he found me. In 1 Peter 2:9, we read, "But you are chosen people, a royal priesthood, a holy nation, God's special possession, that you may declare the praises of him who called you out of darkness into his wonderful light." He determined me to be royalty, a holy and very distinguished possession. Can you imagine that? Peter wrote that we were to broadcast the praises of the one who called us out of darkness into his wonderful light.

In Isaiah 43:1, we read, "Do not be afraid, for I have ransomed you. I have called you by name; you are mine." He has called me by name, and I am his. My name, Zanthia, means beautiful flower— she dares excel and is a bridge over troubled water. I never used to like my name; when I was a child, I was sometimes embarrassed to introduce myself. My mom had gotten my name out of a book; she found all her children's names in books, but for a long time, I never knew the meaning of mine. The day I learned its meaning, much changed for me. That was in 1998. Someone wanted me to sell key rings personalized with names. I made a deal with the person: if he could find out the meaning of my name, I'd sell his keyrings. Two weeks later, he came back with the meaning.

The psalmist wrote, "You saw me before I was born. Every day of my life was recorded in your book. Every moment was laid out before a single day had passed" (Psalm 139:16). Why should I worry about tomorrow or the future when God has my life all laid out for me? He knew everything about me: my name, all my family, my strengths and weaknesses, my failures and successes—everything. Nothing about me is a surprise to him. As the psalmist sang to God, "You made all the delicate, inner parts of my body and knit me together in my mother's womb. Thank you for making me so wonderfully complex! Your workmanship is marvelous—how well I know it" (Psalm 139:13).

Everything about me has been beautifully put together. I am just as God planned and made me to be. There is only one me. There is no copy of me walking about somewhere else. My gifts, talents, character, and DNA are unique to me. Nobody can do what I do because I handle life in my own way.

What an amazing truth! How awesome is our God that he would bestow such lavishness upon us! He wanted to have relationships with us from the beginning. That's our birthright as his children. He has brought me into sonship: "God decided in advance to adopt us into his own family by bringing us to himself through Jesus Christ" (Ephesians 1:5). We are to live out this truth every day for the rest of our lives. My identity is locked in what Jesus did for me when he died for my sins—a beautiful gift packaged with so much love, grace, mercy, and value. We should never underestimate the value of this gift. As we grow in our love, knowledge, and understanding of Jesus, this gift becomes even more of a treasure; we cannot imagine our lives without it. As our understanding of this precious gift of redemption and righteousness increases, our view of everything about us and around us will change.

Each day, I strive to live out of the knowledge that Christ lives inside me. It is no longer I who live but Christ—the hope of glory. Given who I was and who I am now, I thank God every day for saving me from myself. I shudder when I think what my life could have been like without him. I am a vehicle for Christ carrying love, grace, and mercy to the world. I am his footprints here on earth, and where I go, he goes.

Jeremiah prophesied, "I have loved you with an everlasting love, I have drawn you with unfailing kindness" (Jeremiah 31:3 NIV). He loves me! I have many favorite verses, but this one makes me cry every time I read it. His kindness leads us to repent (Romans 2:4). This verse provided the inspiration for the chorus of a beautiful song by Leslie Phillips.

It's your kindness that leads us
To repentance Oh Lord
Knowing that You love us
No matter what we do
Makes us want to love You too.

My Story

How did I get my identity in Christ? Like so many others, I struggled to find my identity in him. You will experience my journey in discovering who I am in this book.

I was aware of God's tugging at my heart for a long time, but I always shifted it to the side, thinking, *Maybe one day I'll do it.* It took me twelve years to make that decision. In those twelve years, a lot of unnecessary stuff happened. I was twelve when I had an encounter with the Holy Spirit at a youth meeting in our Anglican congregation. That night's experience

> "I have loved you with an everlasting love, I have drawn you with unfailing kindness."
> —Jeremiah 31:3

stayed with me, and many times, I wanted to and prayed the sinner's prayer on Sunday nights while sitting in front of the television. Even so, I would find myself back in my old reality the next morning. Back then, Sunday television programs broadcast mostly Christian content. It helps to remember that this was my journey. You can get saved anywhere and in any situation.

I was twenty-four when I officially and publicly made that decision in a small congregation. It was only through my public commitment that I felt assured I had been born again. I was baptized five months later. All I knew then was that I had made a decision to follow Jesus, and I was certain I wanted to be a follower of Christ in the real sense of the word. I wanted to be a good, obedient, and persevering Christian. I wanted to grow in my relationship with God. The next day, I bought the New King James Version of the Bible because it was easy to read and understand.

Today, we have a wider range of versions to choose from. For ten years now, I have been reading the New Living Translation. I started reading it every day. I didn't understand many things, but I knew deep in my heart that this was the one thing in my life I would see through. For my whole life, I was made to believe that I couldn't achieve what I set out to do, that I wasn't smart enough. I was a quitter. Thank God my self-perception changed. I have the privilege now to be whom God says I am and to live in the fullness of Christ.

5

Chapter 2

I Am Loved by God

I have loved you, my people, with an everlasting love.
With unfailing love, I have drawn you to myself.
—Jeremiah 31:3

A golden thread called love runs all through the Bible. Creation was an act of love so great and unconditional and yet so amazing that we Christians often struggle to come to terms with it and others never get to understand it. John 3:16 reads, "God so loved the world that He gave His one and only Son, that whoever believes in Him shall not perish but have eternal life." No matter your situation or state of mind, if you believe in him, you will have eternal life.

God loves me, and he has chosen me to be his very own. In Jeremiah 1:5, we read, "Before I formed you in the womb I knew you," and in Psalm 139:13, we learn, "He created my inmost being, he knitted me together in my mother's womb." These two verses clearly indicate the epitome of his love and how personal he is. He knew everything about me before I was made. He personally knitted me together in every detail. He made me short and gave me a beautiful smile to mention just some of the great assets God blessed me with. He has put purpose and potential in me. He has made me the head, not the tail (Deuteronomy 28:13).

I am fearfully and wonderfully made. I am created in the image of God. God loves me, and I am deserving of His love. I am who God says I am and who he intended me to be. In Isaiah 49:15–16, we read, "I would not forget you! See, I have written your name on the palms of my hands." Psalm 139:1 says, "He examined my heart and knows everything about me and everything I do." He searches my heart to see what's in it; he knows everything about me. I cannot hide from him. I encourage you to read Psalm 139. He has always had his hands firmly wrapped around me; his eye has always been upon me.

It's not about what people say or think about me; it's about God's opinion of me. We all come from somewhere, but that doesn't define who we are. Isaiah 55:8: "'My thoughts are nothing like your thoughts,' says the Lord. 'And my ways are far beyond anything you could imagine.'" God operates from a different perspective; we should view ourselves as God does.

It doesn't matter how you came to be where you are; God chose you to be the person you are. You are his most-prized workmanship, his handiwork. You are loved by God. The most-prized gift you will ever receive is the love of our Father.

My Story

For a long time, I felt disconnected from the truth that God so loved me he sent Jesus to die for me. I was not sure of who I was and who I was meant to be. That lack of knowledge and understanding occupied me for years. I wanted to experience and know that love deep inside. But still, I was serious in my pursuit with God.

I had to first confront the love of God that led Jesus to die on the cross. When I first accepted Christ, I didn't fully comprehend this act of love. I knew I wanted to make this decision, but I didn't understand the price Jesus had paid for me personally; it was more head knowledge than heart knowledge. Until it became an issue of my heart, I couldn't experience, embrace, and accept his love. I gradually came to understand and experience his love for me.

As I paged through my journals of over twenty years, I saw the fine line of love growing year in and year out. I experienced God's love and grew in my love for and understanding and knowledge of him.

> "O Lord, you have examined my heart and know everything about me."
> —Psalm 139:1

Yet there came a time when I longed for a deeper love for him. I began to pray every day that God would allow me to grow in my love for him in a way I hadn't experienced before. I wanted a love that would allow me to be in awe of him every day, a burning love that would bring me to tears for the rest of my life. I never want to feel complacent in my love for him. And it happened for me. I still pray that same prayer every day: "Lord, I want to grow in my love for you and others. I want to live in awe of you every day."

A Journal Extract

8/2/14

Father, I thank you for your work in my life. The privilege to serve in your body. God, you have a plan and purpose for my life, and I am so expectant to follow and see what more you have for me. I love you, Lord, and I want to grow in my love for you each day.

Each day, Lord, I want be in awe of you and fascinated by you. I want to make difference in the world around me. I want to grow deeper in my knowledge of you so I can be used by you in great ways and leave a lasting impression of you in the lives of people around me and all over the world. I am so humbled by the thought that you are increasing in my life that I often wonder if I am worthy to have so much of you inside me. And why me, Lord? I humbly wait for your answer.

Oh God, you are so good and great. Words cannot express how I feel; I can only cry in the thought of who you are, I love you, Lord. I have left my many mistakes and failures behind me. And God, did I learn valuables lessons! My Lord, help me use all these as valuable lessons and testimonies to strengthen, encourage others, and leave a legacy.

My biggest ministry is to my family. Help me be an example of hope light to my family and never giving up on any situation or anyone. Help me persevere in prayer and faith and believe in you for the impossible to be possible in their lives.

God, my desire is that they enjoy the fullness and greatness of who you are and flourish in their relationships with you and accomplish great things for you.

Glory and honor to you, my King and Savior, Jesus.

Chapter 3

I Am Accepted and Chosen by God

Just as love was from the beginning the motive, so is acceptance. You cannot have one without the other. Where there is love, there will be acceptance. "Therefore, accept each other just as Christ has accepted you so that God will be given glory" (Romans 15:7). "God has accepted me, just as I am". (Psalm 27:10 NIV) "Though my father and mother forsake me, the Lord will receive me".

He has embraced and accepted me. Come as you are. No matter who you are or what state you're in, come!

> Come to me, all of you who are weary and carry heavy burdens, and I will give you rest. Take my yoke upon you. Let me teach you, because I am humble and gentle at heart, and you will find rest for your souls. For my yoke is easy to bear, and the burden I give you is light. (Matthew 11:28–30)

I am inspired by the story of the two criminals who were crucified with Jesus. One belittled Jesus, but the other was humble; he knew who Jesus was. He had nothing to lose; he took the chance and asked Jesus to remember him when he went to his kingdom. Jesus responded, "I assure you, today you will be with me in paradise" (Luke 23:39–43). A beautiful example of acceptance.

The opposite of acceptance is rejection. We all fear being rejected for not being smart, fashionable—the list goes on and on. We live in a world in which a false concept and understanding of acceptance is portrayed. It requires us be brand orientated, to dress a certain way, and to act in a certain way to be accepted. We end up trying to live up to others' standards so we will be accepted. We often do things that don't align with our values let alone what we can afford. Romans 12:2 tells us, "Do not conform to the pattern of this world." If our identities are not firmly rooted in Jesus, we will give in to the pressures of this world.

> Just as He chose us in Him before the foundation of the world, that we should be holy and without blame before him in love, having predestined us to adoption as sons by Jesus Christ to Himself, according to the good pleasure of His will, to the praise of the glory of His grace, by which He made us accepted in the beloved. (Ephesians 1:4–6 NKJV)

In this verse, we read four amazing truths about us. First, we have been chosen before the foundations of the world. Second, we have been predestined. God's destiny for me was to be his daughter and have a purpose for my life. Third, we have been adopted into his marvelous family. Fourth, we have been accepted; we are highly favored and were created for his pleasure. Jeremiah 29:11 says, "'For I know the plans I have for you,' declares the Lord, 'plans to prosper you and not to harm you, plans to give you hope and a future.'" Since we were chosen, God has a plan and a purpose for our lives. I hold onto this foundational truth every day in every situation.

My Story

A few weeks after attending a church, the people there would ask me whether I was ready to make a commitment to the Lord. I said that I wasn't ready, that I needed to sort out many things in my life first. I believed I needed to get good first. What a lie!

For a while, I held onto this false understanding that God accepted only good people who did good in the sight of people. Again, a false belief. Not long after that, I decided to invite Jesus into my heart. I realized it was not about getting good first, that idea was based on the Law. Yet over the years in my walk with him, I noticed my relationship was driven by musts—

> "However, those the Father has given me will come to me, and I will never reject them."
> —John 6:37

must go, must do, must behave, must act. There are no such musts when it comes to following Christ. I acted out of the need to please others, not from wanting to. My identity was tied up in the acceptance of others. I would serve on teams knowing my heart wasn't in it. But how could I say no? If my heart had to be in the right place, I would feel no pressure to perform or impress others to gain recognition. When I confronted the musts, I became more free in my relationship with Jesus and without the pressure to perform and be good. I serve now, go to church, and volunteer because I want to, not to avoid guilt for not doing so. I've found that it is okay to say no, to tell others confidently and honestly that I'm tired and need a rest.

God expects nothing more from us than a pure heart and our devotion to him. Nothing I do will make God love me more. "Obviously, I'm not trying to win the approval of people, but of God. If pleasing people were my goal, I would not be Christ's servant" (Galatians 1:10). I cannot impress God by doing this or that. He knows my heart and accepts me just as I am.

Chapter 4

I Have Been Forgiven by God

> Forgiveness is the final form of love
> —Reinhold Niebuhr

We thank you, Lord, for choosing the way our Father set out for you to go. You acted in obedience so we could be made whole and restored in fellowship with our Father. In humbleness, you took on our sins, endured pain, and shed your blood to heal us. Your hanging on the cross displayed the great love of our Father. History was transformed by your great act of love never to be the same.

I love Hebrews 8, one my favorite passages in the New Testament. The heading reads, "The new covenant is greater than the old." Verse 6 reads, "But now Jesus, our High Priest, has been given a ministry that is far superior to the old priesthood, for he is the one who mediates for us a far better covenant with God, based on better promises." Doesn't this verse make you jump and shout for joy? This is truly marvelous.

> "As far as the east is from the west, so far has he removed our transgressions from us."
> —Psalm 103:12

We got a better deal and greater promises as well. Why would we want to pass up an opportunity like that? Is says that the first

13

covenant was faulty so God had to come up with a better one. Verse 10 reads, "But this the new covenant I will make with the people of Israel on that day, says the Lord: I will put my laws in their minds, and I will write them on their hearts. I will be their God, and they will be my people."

The external laws inscribed on stone tablets were replaced with the internal law—it is inside of us; our minds and hearts. It is now part of our new nature.

Accepting God's Forgiveness

Through this new covenant, we have gained right standing with God and the forgiveness of our sins. Herein lies our freedom; this is what it's all about. Christ offered his body so we would be free of our sins. God sent Jesus to buy us back to himself. This is awesome! God always wanted us for himself; that was his plan from the beginning.

How could my sin be forgiven just like that? A lifetime of wrongdoing, wrong living, is just gone. I am now washed clean—no spot of dirt. Many believers have lived and some are still living in the shadows of grace of undeserved forgiveness and rob themselves of the freedom of redemption and the gift of forgiveness. No matter what your sin is, how big or how bad, you are forgiven.

Isaiah 43:25 (NIV) reads, "I, even I, am he who blots out your transgressions, for my own sake, and remembers your sins no more." Because we, being human, do not forget, we tend to think God wouldn't forget either. It says clearly he is a sovereign God. Isaiah 1:18 (NIV) tells us, "Though your sins are like scarlet, they shall be as white as snow; though they are red as crimson, they shall be like wool." And Psalm 103:12 (NIV) tells us, "As far as the east is from the west, so far has he removed our transgressions from us."

There is no account of our wrongdoing anymore. It has been blotted out; there is no evidence of it. God does not remember our sins, our wrongdoings, the injustices we committed; whatever our sins might have been, they don't exist on God's records anymore. Hebrews 10:17: "I will never again remember their sins and lawlessness deeds." John 8:36: "So if the Son sets you free, you will be free indeed." Colossians 1:13–14: "For he has rescued us from the kingdom of darkness and transferred us into the kingdom of his dear Son, who purchased our freedom and forgave our sins." Christ bought us with his death on the cross so we could be free from the claws of the kingdom of darkness.

Because we feel unworthy, we struggle to process this for we cannot fully embrace nor understand the true meaning thereof; that all our sins have been forgiven.

> When you were dead in your sins and in the uncircumcision of your flesh, God made you alive with Christ. He forgave us all our sins, having canceled the charge of our legal indebtedness, which stood against us and condemned us, he has taken it away, nailing it to the cross. (Colossians 2:13–14 NIV)

My Story

It took me a long time to overcome yet another false belief on the forgiveness of my sins. I remember confessing my sins many times. When I was reminded of a past sin, I would pray again for forgiveness. When things would go wrong in my life, I would think it could be due to an unrepented sin. It was as if I couldn't do enough confessing just in case God didn't get it the first time; I wanted to make sure my slate was clean. I lived in shame and condemnation. I struggled with the idea of my sins being wiped completely away. I thought there must be punishment. The Law requires punishment for

> "Though your sins are like scarlet, they shall be as white as snow; though they are red as crimson, they shall be like wool."
> —Isaiah 1:18

15

sin; we don't just forgive somebody like that let alone forget the injustice committed. We naturally tend to make others feel the pain they have inflicted on us, but God doesn't operate that way. He is a just God who sent Jesus to make a new covenant of love and redeem us from our sins. What freedom is in this truth! When I started living out of this truth, I felt free and joyous.

I love snow's beautiful whiteness and purity. I'd stare at it and think, *Jesus removed all my sin, and I am now as white as snow. All the dirt and rubble is gone and covered by his blood.* I'm overwhelmed when I stand in snow; a reality check takes place. *Wow! I'm as white as snow.*

Dealing with Guilt, Self-Condemnation, and Forgiving Ourselves

Guilt and condemnation are other obstacles keeping us from living in the fullness of forgiveness. We feel guilty when we feel condemned for something we did and feel we have not been forgiven for. Many believers live with guilt for something they did and that they feel is unpardonable. And if no one knows about it, the guilt can be worse, often causing chronic disease. Isaiah 54:4 (NIV): "Do not be afraid; you will not be put to shame. Do not fear disgrace; you will not be humiliated. You will forget the shame of your youth and remember no more the reproach of your widowhood."

My Story

When I started out in business, I soon learned being nice wouldn't get me anywhere; I learned new habits so I could survive in the business world. I became someone I didn't like; I was nice to my customers but hard, cold, and sometimes mean to my colleagues and suppliers. That made me feel guilty, but I kept up that behavior. Finally, I wasn't enjoying my work. It was years later that I decided to change and take back the person I used to be. This was all part of the process I'll explain in later chapters.

Only by accepting God's forgiveness can we forgive ourselves for the wrongs we've done to others. This is hard for many, and this has kept many in bondage. The enemy, the deceiver, the father of lies makes us believe we're unworthy of forgiveness and makes us doubt God could forgive us when we are unable to forgive ourselves. We live and behave out of feelings of unworthiness. When we accept God's forgiveness and forgive ourselves, we can live in the freedom of the cross.

John 8:36 reads, "So if the Son sets you free, you will be free indeed." I am truly free, no longer in bondage. Not too long ago, I talked about this with two people who had committed crimes and were facing punishment. They were willing to take the consequences for their deeds, but they struggled with accepting God's forgiveness and forgiving themselves. I told them that though society had passed judgements, God had forgiven them. By accepting God's forgiveness and forgiving themselves, they would find the freedom to take responsibility for their actions in the right attitude of heart. Romans 8:1: "So now there is no condemnation for those who belong to Christ Jesus."

> "So if the Son sets you free, you will be free indeed."
> —John 8:36

We are innocent. No charge can be laid against us. I don't have to look over my shoulder anymore. I don't have to carry guilt anymore because it has been nailed to the cross. It is gone and forgotten. Accept that.

If you haven't yet invited Christ into your life, now is the opportunity. Romans 10:13 tells us, "For everyone who calls on the name of the Lord will be saved." Say this prayer: "Heavenly Father, I thank you for Jesus, who chose to die for me. I ask you to forgive my sins. I ask Jesus to come into my heart and to be Lord of my life. Thank you for giving me eternal life, in Jesus's name, amen."

Congratulations! You are now born again!

Chapter 5

I Am a New Creation

It is a new beginning. I have new dreams to dream. I have a new vision and purpose for my life. Hope is restored. My journey to eternal life has begun. In 2 Corinthians 5:17, we read, "This means that anyone who belongs to Christ has become a new person. The old life is gone; a new life has begun!" This verse is one of the most important in the New Testament. The rubber hits the road here. This verse says it all and sets the record straight just in case you didn't fully understand what the consequences were of the choice you made to be a follower of Christ. Many hardly pay attention and some don't pay attention at all to this verse, which should be underlined and boldfaced in every Bible. We have to think deep and thoroughly to understand what it means. I love this verse; it is my claim to victory.

Let's look at the story in John 3. Nicodemus asked Jesus how someone could be born again. He said, "Surely they cannot enter a second time into their mother's womb to be born!" Jesus answered, "Very truly I tell you, no one can enter the kingdom of God unless they are born of water and the Spirit." Flesh gives birth to flesh, but the Spirit gives birth to spirit. A spiritual rebirth took place.

I have been born anew! Jesus took away my sins and all my hurt, pain, disappointments, failures—everything—and I am new and whole. Can you accept that gift? Did you fully grasp the consequences of this decision, the greatest decision you ever made? And this is where we all get stuck. The sooner we embrace this truth, the sooner we will move on to the next stage and grow. Many stay spiritually infants because they don't understand this verse. Here, we get the opportunity to leave behind everything that would hinder our journey and our growth; we leave it at the foot of the cross. Our past is behind us, and we look forward to our new lives in Christ Jesus.

Imagine a computer with a hard drive that is filled with junk. You delete everything on it and install a new operating system and new programs. It's still has its old shell, but it's now refurbished. There are no traces of the old files. But we feel handicapped with the new; we wish we could go back to our old ways of doing things, the familiar environment, on our unrefurbished computer. But think of it this way. The new operating system installed is now Jesus in you. He is the new operator of your life. You are now the vehicle that is transporting Christ.

> "This means that anyone who belongs to Christ has become a new person. The old life is gone; a new life has begun!"
> —2 Corinthians 5:17

It's hard work. It takes intention and determination, and you feel you don't have that. Rest assured, this is a process, and all processes take time. Having to free yourself of the old self might seem impossible, but believe me, it isn't. If you want to be free of your old self, you've won half the battle already. That may sound insensitive and hard to handle.

Our biggest problem in overcoming the old self is having to change our belief systems. We come out of a worldly belief system and into a Christlike belief system, but that takes effort. Many of us coming from Christian backgrounds have belief systems that don't add up to the one Christ wants us to have; I think many of us believers are still trapped in old belief systems. We've been programmed by our parents and others from the day we were born to think about God and the world around us in a certain way. We have been taught that God sits on a throne waiting for us to do something wrong so he can punish us. Many cannot relate to God as a loving Father because our beliefs were tarnished by the words and deeds of our earthly fathers. When we come to Christ, all these false beliefs will change as we are transformed into the new person.

We have to accept this and the other truths mentioned earlier if we want to flourish as believers. Titus 3:5 tells us, "He saved us, not because of the righteous things we have done but because of is mercy. He washed away our sins, giving us a new birth and new life through the Holy Spirit." How wonderful is this? God did something for us and gave something to us no one else could.

> "No, dear brothers and sisters, I have not achieved it, but I focus on this one thing: Forgetting the past and looking forward to what lies ahead."
> —Philippians 3:13

We all have stories to tell; we all went through trauma, terrible things inflicted upon us, loved ones betraying us, and so on. I'm in no way trivializing what we have gone through. I've gone through pain. I had some mom issues, I had an alcoholic dad, I went through betrayal, but I made a decision years ago that my past would not define my future or keep me from living and enjoying what Christ had for me.

I started embracing my past and renewing some beliefs. I chose to live in gratitude to God for using my past to draw me to himself and to enjoy a fulfilled life free from my past. In my walk with him over the last twenty-six years, I have made many mistakes and countless bad choices due to a wrong belief system. I have accepted the consequences and embraced the truth, and I'm learning important lessons along the way. I choose every day to forget what is behind and look at what is ahead of me. This doesn't happen overnight; it's a process of pursuing God and wanting to live the way he wants us to. We can avoid veering off our paths by truly accepting and embracing the fact that we are new creations. Through Jesus's death on the cross, God sends us forgiveness, wholeness, newness, and new births.

Romans 8:28 says,

> We know that God causes everything to work together for the good of those who love God are called according to his purpose from them. For God knew his people in advance, and he chose them to become like His Son, so that his Son would be the firstborn.

He knew the journey my life would make. He chose me to become his daughter. This verse remains one of my pillar verses, one I lean on when I face trials. Further down in Romans 8 is another profound piece I'd like to share with you.

My Story

When I was about four years young in my walk with God, everyone in my little congregation was asked to take some counseling sessions. I was confused. I didn't understand why I had to relive and share my traumatic experiences. Some in our congregation experienced some kind of breakthroughs, but not me. I didn't feel the need for counseling though I had some stuff I had to work through, but counseling about it wasn't relevant to me then.

But as I grew in my walk with God, I became aware of certain behaviors and mind-sets that weren't serving me well. I thought about them and could link them to experiences I'd had. One such incident was having to repeat a year in school, which I'll write about later. I started talking through these things with God—how I felt at the time it had happened—and then ask him to heal and restore that area of my life.

Getting over ourselves is a process we should be willing to undertake. Here and there, I find little behaviors that just aren't Christlike. I call that sweeping the rooms of my heart. We sometimes store garbage in our hearts without knowing that. It's only when we consciously search the rooms of our hearts that we discover some things are out of place. After reflection, we can get to the root of the issue.

Invite the Holy Spirit to lead you and show you those areas. To confront them and let them go takes courage, but I assure you,

> "But he was pierced for our rebellion, crushed for our sins, He was beaten so we could be whole. He was whipped so we could be healed."
> —Isaiah 53:5

it will be worth it. We should never allow the trauma we have experienced to frame our identity. Scripture tells us our sorrows weighed Jesus down; he was beaten so we could become whole. We are healed through his stripes (Isaiah 53:4–5). I am thankful that God allowed me to live unattached from my past.

I do not mean to downgrade counseling; I have a high regard for this ministry and for the work counselors do, and I have empathy for those who seek such help to get back on their feet. Many cannot do this by themselves and need a counselor to help them heal. I have counseled others during difficult times in their lives. Psalm 147:3 reads, "He heals the brokenhearted and bandages their wounds." Only God can heal and restore our broken hearts.

I was confused about having to go through something Christ had already dealt with. What I didn't know was that I had to unlearn and let go of some things that happened to me and subsequently influenced my behaviors. Feelings of rejection, insecurity, and anger can lurk in the corners of our hearts waiting to jump out the moment we face pressure or confrontation. We are a product of our pasts, right? I asked God to clarify this for me as I believed all there was to my life had been sorted out at the cross. I fought with this for weeks, but then, he showed me Romans 8:33–34/38–39.

Who dares accuse us whom God has chosen for his own? No one—for God himself has given us right standing with himself. Who then will condemn us? No one—for Christ Jesus died for us and was raised to life for us, and he is sitting in the place of honor at Gods right hand, pleading for us.

And I am convinced that nothing can ever separate us from Gods love. Neither death nor life, neither angels nor demons, neither our fears for today nor our worries about tomorrow – not even the powers of hell can separate us from God's love. No power in the sky above or in the earth below—indeed, nothing in all creation will ever be able to separate us from the love of God that is revealed in Christ Jesus our Lord.

Through these verses, God showed me nothing could separate us from his love. The word *past* is not there because the past doesn't matter, it has no influence or power. In God's view, our past doesn't exist anymore. Does this mean God is insensitive to our past? No. Psalm 56:8 tells us, "You have taken account of my wanderings; put my tears in your bottle and are they not in your book?" Isn't that assuring? My deepest sorrows and pains have not been overlooked. He has collected all my tears and recorded them all. I was relieved to know I could do nothing to gain God's stamp of approval other than living in the acceptance of what he has done for me.

> "You have taken account of my wanderings; put my tears in your bottle and are they not in your book."
> —Psalm 56:8

In Philippians 3:13, Paul wrote, "No, dear brothers and sisters, I have not achieved it, but I focus on this one thing: Forgetting the past and looking forward to what lies ahead." That's a sobering and encouraging verse. We should live in the now and the future. We strip ourselves of God's blessing and abundance when we live in the old and not embrace the new. Deuteronomy 30:19 says, "Today I have given you the choice between life and death, between blessings and curses. Now I call on heaven and earth to witness the choice you make. Oh, that you would choose life, so that you and your descendants might live!"

Choose today to be free from your past and grab the blessings, the freedom, and the wholeness God has for you.

Part 2

Part 2

Chapter 6

Renewing Your Mind

> You must learn a new way to think before
> you can master a new way to be.
> —Marianne Williamson

To live as a new creation, you must keep your refurbished computer in good order by installing new programs and a new operating system. You have to give up your old ones. You have to delete old thoughts and install new thoughts if you want to live a victorious life. Nothing will happen by itself; it will take effort and discipline. How else will you be able to offer yourself as a living, holy sacrifice? Romans 12:1 tells us, "I plead with you to give your bodies to God because of all he has done for you. Let them be a living a holy sacrifice—the kind he will find acceptable. This is truly the way to worship him."

We change ourselves because of what he has done for us and who he is. Jesus deserves our best. We can transform our lives for his glory. It's out of gratitude that we do what pleases him. We aren't forced to do anything; we allow God to transform us because we identified ourselves with his death on the cross.

Romans 12:2 says, "Don't copy the behavior and customs of this world, but let God transform you into a new person by changing the way you. Then you will learn to know Gods will for you, which is good and pleasing and perfect." We are to become different people who look and act different from the way the world does. We are to be transformed into the new creation, and this can happen only through renewing our minds and right thinking. We are in this world but not of this world (John 17:16). We see, hear, and experience the world but are to distance ourselves from it so it will not affect us.

> "Then the way you live will always honor and please the Lord, and your lives will produce every kind of good fruit. All the while, you will and you learn to know God better and better."
> —Colossians 1:10

This world is only our temporary home. We changed through our conversion, and a spiritual rebirth took place. We are to be different from whatever we were before. Our minds and hearts have to be renewed. The process of dying to self, letting go of our old nature, and becoming Christlike sanctifies us. Our minds are to be filled with the knowledge of Christ and his will so we will have spiritual wisdom and understanding and so our lives will honor and please him. That's the way we will bring forth good fruit (Colossians 1:9–10).

Yet many are stuck in between; they want the best of both worlds. This is because many have not yet identified themselves fully with the work of the cross and accepted the change that needs to take place. Until we find our true identity in Christ, we will live short of the blessings and abundance he intends us to have.

Most seem to have a misunderstanding of grace. It's almost a kind of message that says we don't have to change, we can come as we are and stay as we are. Jesus died for all mankind—regardless of who we are or what we have done, we can come as we are. However, the cross does require us to change. We have to transform in the way we think and behave; we cannot behave the way the world wants us to and expect the world to follow our lead. That mind-set is not true Christianity; no rebirth took place in that instance. Grace is not a license to sin as many seem to believe. God hates sin, and so should we. We have been made to believe through religion that though we are born again, we are still sinners. That is false. We read in Romans 6:6–7, "We know that our old sinful selves were crucified with Christ so that sin might lose its power in our lives. We are no longer slaves to sin. For when we died with Christ we were set free from the power of sin." We read in 1 John 3:5–6, "And you know that Jesus came to take away our sins, and there is no sin in him. Anyone who continues to live in him will not sin. But anyone who keeps on sinning does not know him or understand who he is."

We are free from the clutches of our sinful nature. Our new nature is Christlike. We can understand the true, deep meaning of grace only after we fully grasp the work of the cross. Grace came at the highest price ever anyone could pay so we could have life eternal.

> "Throw off your old sinful nature and your former way of life, which is corrupted by lust and deception. Instead, let the spirit renew your thoughts and attitudes. Put on your new nature, created to be like God, truly righteous and holy."
> —Ephesians 4:22–23

The second part of Romans 12:2 instructs to transform ourselves by renewing our minds. We are to let God change our character, our nature, and our condition. The word *transform* also means convert. We convert into the new person through right thinking. We have to lay down a new belief system and habits. Colossians 3:10 says, "Put on your new nature, and be renewed as you learn to know your creator and become like him." In neuroscience, this process is called rewiring of the brain through creating new pathways or memories. We have to feed in new information and think new thoughts that fit our new

> "Study this Book of Instruction continually. Meditate on it day and night so you will be sure to obey everything written in it. Only then will you prosper and succeed in all you do."
> —Joshua 1:8

identities. The old system will not serve us well in our new identity. This is hard work we will not complete in a week, a month, or a year. Becoming sanctified is a lifelong process we have to undertake with intention and discipline. We have deep-rooted behaviors and habits that will not work with our new identities; we have to intentionally change them. According to neuroscientists, it takes up to a month to change a habit. Think of how many bad habits we have to change.

James 1:4 tells us, "So let it grow, for when your endurance is fully developed, you will be perfect and complete, lacking nothing." The sooner we get to start laying down the new pathways, the sooner we will start reaping results. Christians can change their mind-sets by reading and meditating on the Word of God, praying, and fellowshipping with like-minded people in church. They will come to know God better and better every day.

My Story

After I got a Bible after my conversion, I began reading every day. I wanted to cultivate a habit, a discipline. I was told to start reading the Gospels, so I started with Matthew. That wasn't good advice; I really struggled to focus and understand. (Later, I learned I should have started with Mark). But I kept reading. Though I wasn't getting much out of it, some things stuck. I read and studied as well in home groups. That was helpful; I learned more about scripture in its context, and discussions were very insightful.

At one point, I stopped reading the Bible, but I soon discovered the importance of God's Word and growing in my understanding of him. I prayed about it. I asked God to give me a hunger and thirst for his Word. God did that, and I started to read again because I wanted to understand his Word. It went slowly, but I kept at it. When I started reading the Bible from the beginning, it became more exciting. The stories intrigued me, and I couldn't stop.

Many years later, I still hunger and thirst for God's Word, and the more I walk with him, the more I understand it. I continually discover truths that transform my life. I never liked reading the Bible on electronic devices because I loved to underline verses, but I've learned I can do that on my device and do so in different colors and search for and find them quickly. I've grown to love my Bible app, especially the audio part—I listen to it when I'm cooking, eating, bathing, and at night before I fall asleep. Trust me—that's a soothing way to fall asleep.

Chapter 7

How Does the Mind Work?

A man's mind may be likened to a garden, which may be
intelligently cultivated or allowed to run wild; but whether
cultivated or neglected, it must, and will, bring forth. If no
useful seeds are put into it, then an abundance of useless weed-
seeds will fall therein, and will continue to produce their kind.

—James Allen

Due to constant new studies and research on the brain, we learn
now from science that our brain is not hardwired; it can be rewired
due to our brains' neuroplasticity. Our neurons transmit nerve
signals to and from the brain. Plasticity refers to our brains' ability
to change, modify, adapt, and regrow.

Our brain has the potential to create new cells and neural
pathways as needed. We can call on our brains to exercise their
inherent neuroplasticity by trying to learn new things, but this
requires practice and repetition, and that requires intention.

Our minds are the most powerful tool in the universe outside
of God, and we can use them constructively or destructively. As the
Holy Spirit lives in us, we have the power to change our brains for
the better. We need to create environments for our minds to produce
what we intend to bring forth. We need to pull out all the weeds in

our minds before we can plant new seeds. Old habits have to go before we can develop new habits, and this is a learned skill as is the case with so many things in life. Everything takes time, practice, and repetition, but we can develop new habits and gain mastery in new areas. Think of what goes into a gymnast's success—years of practice. But our brains can handle this; they are capable of making great changes and unlearning bad habits.

> "For I can do everything through Christ, who gives me strength."
> —Philippians 4:13

Ideas to Retrain Our Brains

First, realize you can rewire your brain. Second, establish and identify the beliefs or habits you want to change. Third, write down the new beliefs or truths you want to replace the old with. Find a Bible verse that strengthens your new belief. You will also have to sincerely desire to change, so invite the Holy Spirit to guide you and show you.

We can bring about change in our lives only through the conviction of the Holy Spirit. Acknowledge the effect of the unhealthy or bad habit has on your life, and focus on your new habit. In his book, *Think and Grow Rich,* Napoleon Hill says, "Any idea, plan or purpose may be placed in the mind through repetition of thought." Take thoughts captive when confronted with bad and doubting thoughts. Have a community of friends who can help and support you, or find an accountability partner. Meditate on the Word of God; that's the best way to rewire your brain. Pray continuously, and believe all things are possible through Christ, who strengthen you (Philippians 4:13).

The Conscious and Subconscious

We are body, soul, and spirit. Our souls consist of our conscious and subconscious minds. E. Stanley Jones put it beautifully: "The conscious mind determines the actions, the subconscious mind determines the reactions, and the reactions are just as important as the actions."

The conscious mind is where the will is—the thinking, reasoning, creative part, our present state of mind and the awareness of our environment. The subconscious is where our habits, belief systems, and our bodies' operations reside. Our memory is in our subconscious and is connected to our bodies through the endocrine, nervous, and immune systems. Our thoughts are at most governed by the subconscious mind. It is here that the rewiring needs to take place.

We exercise free will through our conscious minds; our subconscious has no ability to reject something as false and therefore accepts everything as truth. Every thought we reinforce goes into our subconscious, which impacts our behavior. Feelings are therefore expressed through the subconscious mind. Bruce Lipton wrote, "The subconscious mind is like a tape player, until you change the tape, it will not change." Through conscious awareness, we can alter or improve our thoughts. Practicing healthy, quality thoughts will therefore bring about improvements and growth in our walk with God and in all areas of life.

Belief System or Worldview

We tend to be critical of those who don't think as we do or hold the same views as we do, but we have to respect others' beliefs and worldviews. We all have a right to a belief system or a worldview; that is the way we were shaped. Only when we realize our beliefs or worldviews aren't serving us well can we choose to change them; no one should try to force us to change.

A belief is nothing more than a neural pathway, but we can create new neural pathways. We can alter our belief systems if we want to in spite of how we obtained them—from our parents, our environments, our schooling, culture, and so on. We have been programmed to do certain things in a certain way, to believe this rather than that, to determine what is good and what is bad. Our belief systems can be blessings or curses. We all perceive the world differently through our five senses, and we are conditioned to allow the outside world to control our insides, not the other way around. We have to change the inside before we can see the world differently. Unless we retrain or rewire our minds to become like Christ, will we stay in the old nature.

> We ask God to give you complete knowledge of his will and to give you spiritual wisdom and understanding. Then the way you live will always honor and please the Lord and your lives will produce every kind of good fruit. All the while you will grow as you learn to know God better and better. (Colossians 1:9b–10)

As we perceive the world, we react based on our belief systems, which are programmed in our subconscious mind and result in our habitual behavior—our daily routines, the way we do certain things, the way we react to events. Almost all our behavior is habitual (Bruce Lipton). A habit is something we learn through repetition or inherit. According to B R Andrews, "Habits", in the *The American Journal of Psychology* vol. 14, no. 2 (Apr. 1903), "A habit, from the standpoint of psychology, is a more or less fixed way of thinking, willing, or feeling acquired through previous repetition of a mental experience."[1]

> "For God has not given us a spirit of fear and timidity, but of power, love and a sound mind."
> —2 Timothy 1:7

Your unhealthy lifestyle, your tendency to procrastinate, your biting your nails—everything you do that you shouldn't—constitute your

[1] B R Andrews, "Habits", The American Journal of Psychology vol. 14, no. 2 (Apr. 1903.

habits most of which you are unaware of. But you can change them; you don't have to remain a victim of them. You'll want to cultivate and sustain habits that will allow you to live a life that is fruitful and pleasing to God.

In 2 Timothy 1:7, we read, "For God has not given us a spirit of fear and timidity, but of power, love, and a sound mind." The Bible is rich in truth that can aid us in the renewal process. But to change our false belief systems or habits means we'll have to override our reasoning first as it is very much attached to our subconscious. Our reasoning constantly measures new truths by our old beliefs. Determination and repetition will enable us to live in the new life effectively. Neglecting to move from the old to the new will keep us locked up and prevent us from experiencing the fullness in Christ Jesus. Proverbs 4:23: "Guard your heart above all else, for it determines the course of your life."

Once we become new creations, we receive a new view of the world. We understand that through our rebirth, we have been made new and have the mind of Christ. We have a spirit of power that makes us confident that Christ lives in us and that we have a spirit of love and a healthy, fit, secure, and solid mind at our disposal. If we are afraid, it's for fear of punishment, but this is one ingrained belief we can definitely free ourselves of. Fear keeps us from leaving the familiar for the new. Fear thoughts keep us from taking the steps to bring about change in our lives.

Dr. Caroline Leaf has done great work in her research on the brain. In her books *Switch on your Brian* and *The Gift in You*, she cited countless research and studies on the brain. Her work is concentrated on in-depth studies of the brain and addresses the effects of thoughts. Her books are excellent resources so necessary for us the church today. According to Dr. Leaf and many other neuroscientists, we can change or replace a habit in twenty-one days by spending seven minutes per day on it and another twenty-one days to strengthen the new habit.

My Story

I always believed I wasn't cut out to be a student. I'd start a study program but quit it before finishing. I thought I wasn't as smart or as clever as my siblings were. Where did that come from? I started school when I was five and half. I obviously was not school ready; I failed my first year. That was traumatic; I started off my education hating school. Throughout the rest of my school career, I was at best average. I struggled to achieve the results my two older brothers and my younger sister did, it seemed, naturally. I frequently heard how well they were doing and that I should too.

It was the same story with athletics; I couldn't compete with them. Nobody could accuse me of not trying, but I'd come in last in track, and I always had to play center in netball because I was too short to score let alone contribute to defense. I always imagined myself in the lead role in plays but I was always one of the crowd on stage. I couldn't sing to save my life, but for some reason, I sang every year in the school choir. How I did that is still a mystery. My folks played tennis, but I did manage to compete in table tennis during my high school days. I never finished high school; I opted to go to college. That too was a disaster—I was absent more than I was present.

Throughout my life, I believed I would never master anything. I got off on the wrong foot in first grade, and that affected my whole school career. My false belief in my inadequacies prevented me from achieving what I was capable of. As I discovered who I was and what I was capable of, I replaced my old, false belief system. I committed myself to being a student for the rest of my life.

I now run three to four hours a week. I sing loudly on Sundays, not embarrassed of my voice anymore. I volunteer on our church's moderation team. And yes, I focused all my adult life to grow in my knowledge of God, and I'm pursuing other areas of interest to me as well.

As we face life, as stuff happens to us, we form new belief systems. If we're not careful how we analyze what happens to us and how we deal with these experiences, we'll end up creating false beliefs that won't serve us well. For about two years after our bankruptcy, I believed I'd never run a business again. How could I? After years of struggling, fighting, and hoping that our business would recover from the recession of 2008, we finally had to make the decision to sequestrate. Though I had processed the event and was okay with the idea that business was history for me, I found myself rethinking the whole thing. I had the idea that I was just no good because I had failed miserably. I believed that. But then I would talk to God ...

So it went—every three or four months, I'd visit this place again. I felt my belief wasn't true, but I had to find a way to break out of that thought pattern. As I took a more-intense, personal development path, a light went on. I realized there was more to my life than what I had experienced. On my forty-ninth birthday, God told me to prepare for my fifties and beyond.

Changing my false belief system wasn't a lengthy process. I learned new truths, and even as my doubts would come, I realized and I knew the truth. I started focusing on the promises I had from God.

Chapter 8

Thoughts

It is not what happens to me, it is my
thought to it—my reactions to it.

Our thoughts are in harmony with our belief systems and therefore
shape our behavior. We think good thoughts or bad thoughts but not at
the same time. Thought becomes feelings, feelings become behavior,
and behavior leads to action. To change the result, we need to start with
the way we think; that will reprogram our belief systems. We do this
by deliberate, directed thinking and awareness. It requires repetition.
In his book *The Purpose Driven Life* Rick Warren says, "Repetition is
the mother of character and skill." It's hard work, it takes time and
discipline, but it's not impossible. Rich Warren, *Devotional, We However,
Have the Mind of Christ by Jon Walker, (May 21, 2014).* "When Jesus calls
you, he expects you to begin thinking like him."[2]

Lasting changes come when we choose to think healthy thoughts
that ultimately affect the way we behave. Learning to think like
Jesus isn't as impossible as it sounds. The apostle Paul said that we
have been given the mind of Christ (1 Corinthians 2:16). We must
access the mind of Christ as we meditate on God's Word and listen

---

[2] Rick Warren, Devotional, We However, Have the Mind of Christ by Jon
Walker (May 21, 2014).

to the Holy Spirit, our guide to all truth. As we walk with him day in and day out, we will learn his likes and dislikes. There is no magic solution to this other than having to exercise a Christlike lifestyle.

Luke 6:45 tells us, "A good person produces good things from the treasury of a good heart, and an evil person produces evil things from the treasury of an evil heart. What you say flows from what is in your heart." We will be known by the fruit we bear. We will conform to whatever occupies our minds.

We perceive the world through our senses. As we perceive things based on our belief systems, we think and react in certain ways and bear fruit accordingly. If we want to change the fruit we bear, we will have to change our belief systems, our programming.

Philippians 4:8 tells us, "Dear brothers and sisters, one final thing. Fix your thoughts on what is true, and honorable, and right, and pure, and lovely and admirable. Think about things that are excellent and worthy of praise." We're urged to think on what is good.

We are preoccupied by the events of any one day, and we tend to focus on the bad ones, don't we? The falling out we had with a colleague, the accident we almost got into, right? We're wired to respond to the bad, and the more we think about it, the bigger the issue becomes. We are to exercise self-control, an act of our will, to fix our thoughts on what is true. We will be bombarded with negativity and lies from the enemy, but we can react to the lies or not. In 2 Corinthians 10:5 (NIV), we read, "We demolish arguments and every pretension that sets itself up against the knowledge of God, and we take captive every thought to make it obedient to Christ."

> "W demolish arguments and every pretension that sets itself up against the knowledge of God, and we take captive every thought to make it obedient to Christ."
> —2 Corinthians 10:5

We always have a way out. Refuse to give in to the voices of the enemy. James 4:7 reads, "So humble yourselves before God. Resist the devil, and he will flee from you." We have authority over the enemy and can therefore rebuke and take charge of what is rightfully ours. We are victorious in Christ Jesus. We are no longer victims of our circumstances. We have overcome the enemy.

In 3 John 1:2 (NIV), we read, "Dear friend, I pray that you may enjoy good health and that all may go well with you, even as your soul is getting along well." It is clear that the writer's wish is for the believers to prosper physically and mentally. Everything relies on the state of our souls—our minds. Our thoughts are to line up with the Word of God.

My Story

I always struggled with fear of confrontation and fear of others. In 2009, during a very difficult and challenging time our family was facing, I was driven by fear of what each new day may bring. One Sunday, our pastor gave a sermon about Satan being our real enemy that made me decide to overcome my fear. As I took my morning walk on Monday, I started to pray and declare verses. Psalm 118:6: "The Lord is with me; I will not be afraid. What can mere mortals do to me?" and 2 Timothy 1:7: "for God has not given me a spirit of fear but of power and love and a sound mind" were among them. I prayed that every morning and repeated it as I walked. After two weeks, I felt free of fear. Every time I would be confronted with a situation that caused fear, I'd confront it knowing I could overcome fear. And it happened.

This exercise taught me an important lesson. Desperation drove me to take action, and through believing and declaring God's Word, I was able to experience the release from fear. During this time, I started to practice being aware of my feelings, and that brought about observance of my thoughts.

As a result of the enormous stress I found myself under, my body and hormones were out of balance. Thoughts affect our health. I started listening to my body and making changes for my well-being. I started taking responsibility for my actions when I was not doing well. For example, my husband and I worked together and would often get home at the same time. That meant neither of us had time to "defrost" from our working day; that made it easy for us to get into arguments. But I learned to take time to think how I wanted to react to a situation. This ability saved me from many a mishap. On occasions where I did overstep my boundaries, I could feel the effects of untamed thoughts that resulted in behavior I'd have to repent of later.

On her website, Everyday Answers, under the heading "The Way to Live with the Mind of Christ," Joyce Meyer says, "One of the greatest revelations of my life is: I can choose my thoughts and think things on purpose. In other words, I don't have to just think about whatever falls into my mind." This was a life-changing revelation for her because as Proverbs 23:7 says, "As a man thinks in his heart so is he." She says, where the mind goes, the

> "My dear children, I am writing this to you so that you will not sin. But if anyone does sin, we have an advocate who pleads our case before the Father. He is Jesus Christ, the one who is truly righteous."
> —1 John 2:1

man follows. She is right. We need to understand our identity in Christ and the power we have through him, who lives in us.

We have free will; we need to live in this new mind. I have the mind of Christ. Many Christians think they are sorry little sinners who will never accomplish victory or overcome weaknesses of the flesh. That is wrong. In 1 John 3:9, we read, "Those who have been born into God's family do not make a practice of sinning, because God's life is in them. So they can't keep on sinning, because they are children of God."

It is not in my nature or custom to sin. Nor do I make a habit of sinning. As his seed abides in me, I have no other excuse than to be like him. And if I do sin, I have an advocate, Jesus, who pleads our case before the Father. He is Jesus Christ, the one who is truly righteous (1 John 2:1).

Chapter 9

Practicing Awareness

> The better your awareness, the better your choices. As
> you make better choices, you will see better results.

Most would say that being aware of our thoughts is very difficult, but if I could get it right, so can you. I started practicing becoming aware of my feelings in 2009 without the knowledge I now have. I was desperate for change, and I launched into something I had no idea about. I am so grateful to God for taking me on this journey. I am still growing and learning every day.

Over the last two years, the subject of thought and thinking has drawn me to look into science, particularly neuroscience, and that's when I discovered Dr. Leaf's work. This fascinating subject has given me a deeper understanding of God.

In 2009, when I started taking charge of my body again, I started listening to it. I would pay attention to my feelings. When I sensed fear, I searched for the cause. I then traced it back to my thoughts of fear that would manifest in my body in worry and anxiety. I started to pray and take those unwanted thoughts captive.

By developing a mental awareness of my thoughts, I soon learned to distinguish between good and bad thoughts. God would not send me bad thoughts; those came from Satan. Thoughts become feelings, and feelings become actions or behavior. We act out what we think.

If the Holy Spirit rules your life, you will feed off the Holy Spirit. Likewise, if your fleshly nature rules, you will feed off the flesh. Matthew 7:16 reads, "You can identify them by their fruits, that is, by the way they act. Can you pick grapes from thorn bushes, or figs from thistles?" What is in our hearts will occupy our minds, and we will bring forth whatever is in our hearts. This is the sobering truth. The Bible is clear about that.

> "You can identify them by their fruits, that is, by the way they act. Can you pick grapes from thorn bushes, or figs from thistles?"
> —Matthew 7:16

When we practice awareness of thoughts, we have full control of the results or the fruits we want to bring forth. Isaiah 26:3: "You will keep in perfect peace all who trust in you, all whose thoughts are fixed on you." We can become aware of our thoughts by being aware of our feelings.

Take time to interpret your feelings. What exactly are you feeling? Take them apart, get to the root of the problem, and interpret the cause of the thought. This will take time and involve prayer. You might feel anger, resentment, frustration, doubt, or unforgiveness. Take time to work through those feelings and thoughts and bring the matter to God. Take responsibility for your actions. If you acted unfairly toward someone as a result of your feelings, apologize or ask for forgiveness. Replace the lies or negative thoughts the enemy imposes on you with scripture. This is where the renewing of the mind takes place. The enemy has no authority over you other than the authority you allow him to have. Practice this before going to bed. Make sure you have a good night's rest. Unnecessary, unhealthy thoughts distract the subconscious, and that has a bad effect on the body

God has given us free will; we can believe or not believe. There are only two voices speaking to us—God's and Satan's. Choose which voice you will tune in to. Luke 10:19 tells us, "Look, I have given you authority over all the power of the enemy, and you can walk among snakes and scorpions and crush them. Nothing will injure you."

You can practice awareness in the morning, when your mind is less cluttered—before you check your emails or phone calls—and you can focus on your thoughts and feelings. As I prepare for the day, I am very aware of my state of mind. As I submit my day to God, I become aware of what is in my heart—perhaps it is something left over from yesterday. I will bring those thoughts before God again. When I do that, I find that later in the day, I will discover the issue is gone and I sense peace and freedom.

Practicing awareness at work is difficult. I work in a kindergarten, and as you can imagine, I can get distracted in a second. But when I do get a moment, I reflect on my thoughts. As time went on, I realized that I started to remember my thoughts clearly. I practiced intentionality, which allowed me to stay present for long stretches. I'd feel unsettled after an altercation with a child or a colleague that caught me off guard. After I reflected on the matter, I would realize when I had been out of place and would make amends. Romans 8:33: "Who dares accuse us whom God has chosen for his own? No one—for God himself has given us right standing with himself."

> "Instead, let the spirit renew your thoughts and attitudes."
> —Ephesians 4:23

I live and respond to the conviction of the Holy Spirit and not in condemnation. The enemy is a master in this area; he constantly tries to condemn us for our behavior and actions. We have to take control of our minds by controlling our thoughts. Our minds are our battlefields. We have the power and authority through Jesus to take captive every thought that is counter to the knowledge of God. We cannot blame every wrong action on the enemy; we must take responsibility for our deeds through living in a right state of mind. Being consciously aware is walking in the light and giving the Spirit preference to rule and be expressed. We are to feed off the Spirit; we are to live inwardly, not externally. Allow the Holy Spirit to lead you into all truth and along the right path.

> But you have received the Holy Spirit, and he lives in you, so you don't need anyone to teach you what is true. For the spirit teaches you everything you need to know, and what he teaches is true—it is not a lie. So just as he has taught you, remain in fellowship with Christ. (1 John 2:27)

When we walk in awareness of him, we are open to the promptings of the Holy Spirit and to live in submission to him. When we are self-obsessed, we become driven by the desires of the flesh and have untamed thoughts. Through practicing controlled thought, we avail ourselves of the work of the Holy Spirit in and through us.

John 8:32 says, "You will know the truth and the truth will set you free." We need the knowledge of God so we can transform our thinking and behaving. We will begin speaking his word into every adverse situation. We will live out the knowledge of him through his Word and our relationship with him. Ignorance of the truth will leave us spiritually poor and unable to handle life's challenges. We won't be able to experience God's promises to us.

Part 3

Part 3

Chapter 10

Growing in Him

Of all today's miracles the greatest is this: to know that I find
Thee best when I work listening ... Thank Thee, too, that the
habit of constant conversation grows easier each day. I really
do believe all thought can be conversations with Thee.
—Frank Laubach

A relationship with God demands a changed heart. That requires
action that will transform our lives through him. How we view our
commitments to follow him will affect our relationships with him.
I want to become holy like him. In 1 Peter 1:15, we read, "But now
you must be holy in everything you do, just as God who chose you
is holy."

I will share with you tools and tips that helped me along the way
to finding my identity, growing in God, and living in his abundance.
Jesus cultivated these habits and practiced them every day. In our
pursuit of God, there is no must and no duty; it is purely a matter
of the heart, which seeks a deeper relationship with our Savior, who
has to become the controller of our lives. In 1 Timothy 4:8, we read,
"Physical training is good, but training for godliness is much better,
promising benefits in this life and in the life to come."

Growing requires time, discipline, and sacrifice. We determine the sacrifice we're willing to make to invest in our relationship with him. In 2 Samuel 24, David took a census that displeased God. David's conscience led him to confess his sin and ask God for forgiveness. He had a choice of punishments God would inflict on Israel. David chose a plague, which killed many people. God relented and told the angel of death to stop just as it was by the threshing floor of Araunah the Jebusite.

Later, the prophet Gad told David to build an altar on Araunah's threshing floor. David offered to buy the threshing floor, but Araunah wanted him to have it. Araunah also offered to supply the oxen and wood for the offering. David said, "No, I insist on buying it, for I will not present burnt offerings to the Lord my God that have cost me nothing" (2 Samuel 24:24). Our willingness to make time for God is a sacrifice of something of lesser value for something of higher purpose. The quality and the value of the time we give him depend on the reverence and honor we have for him. As Richard Foster in *Celebration of Discipline* put it, "The primary requirement is a longing after God." When we cultivate a longing for God, we will create the space and time for him. Psalm 42:1 reads, "As the deer longs from streams of water, so I long for you, Oh God. I thirst for God, the living God. When can I go and stand before him?"

Reading the Bible

I believe reading the Bible is one of three pillars of our faith. The second is prayer, and the third is our testimony. We must practice these spiritual disciplines. In Luke 4:16, we read that when Jesus came to Nazareth, his hometown, he would go as usual to the synagogue on the Sabbath and read the scriptures. Romans 10:17: "So faith comes from hearing, that is, hearing the Good news about Christ." It is only right that we give our faith further boosts by reading the Bible to gain more understanding of him and his creation and how we can grow in our relationship with and faith in Him. That takes discipline, time, and sacrifice. Sunday church service is not enough. Matthew 4:4: "People do not live by bread alone, but by every word that comes from the mouth of God." Only when we realize how important this is for our spiritual and emotional well-being will we do what is most important regardless of the price. Reading God's Word every day and believing it increases our faith and brings revelation that leads to change.

> "People do not live by bread alone, but by every word that comes from the mouth of God."
> —Matthew 4:4

Ephesians 4:23 tells us, "Instead, let the spirit renew your thoughts and attitudes." We have everything available to us; we only have to take the action. Since we have the mind of Christ (1 Corinthians 2:16), let us feed off this advantage we have as children of God. This doesn't happen at the snap of a finger; we are also reminded in Philippians 2:5 to have the same mindset of Christ Jesus.

If we fail to cultivate the habit of reading God's Word regularly, we will forever stay stuck between the old and the new. How will we learn God's perfect will for us if we don't read his Word? We are to be mindful that if we don't reject the pressures of the world, we will live as worldly people do. We live in hurried times, everything is instant, but there is unfortunately no instant recipe for spiritual growth; it is a process.

Joshua 1:8 tells us, "Study this Book of Instruction continually. Meditate on it day and night so you will be sure to obey everything written in it. Only then will you prosper and succeed in all you do." Make reading the Bible a priority in your life, by yourself and in groups, and you will reap the benefits and fruit of doing so.

Prayer

Prayer is another pillar of our faith. We believers cannot function without these two vitally important pillars that uphold our faith. If we are to know God, we need to spend time with Him. Prayer is our lifeline to God. Again, this part of our faith is generally neglected due to our tendency to be busy. It requires effort, and for many, it's a battle. We miss out on a great treasure when we miss opportunities to come to Him. Prayer is a gift of grace we received through Christ's death that gave us direct access to the Father. Countless books deal with this subject, as do many booklets. Matthew 6:6 tells us, "But when

> "Make thankfulness your sacrifice to God, and keep the vows you made to the Most High. Then call on me when you are in trouble, and I will rescue you, and you will give me glrory."
> —Psalm 50:14–15

you pray, go away, by yourself, shut the door behind you and pray to your Father in private. Then your Father, who sees everything will reward you."

Prayer has to be a priority for us if we want to grow and know him. This is our most important relationship we will ever have. My prayer times vary, depending on what is on my heart. I enjoy prayer walking, other times I would just want to sit on my couch and talk to God. There are times where I have the need to write my prayers down. Prayer is personal and different for everyone. Find a way that suits you. God so loves it when we sit next to him. My prayers have changed as I grew in my walk with God and my spiritual seasons changed. For the first ten years, my prayers were focused on my marriage, family, and work. I've reread my journals and am embarrassed at how many times I complained to God about my husband and colleagues. Then for many years, my focus was on my business and money. For the last four years, my prayers have been mainly prayers of praise and thanksgiving.

My prayers have also changed for my marriage and children; we have grown older, and life brings different kinds of challenges. My prayers for myself are different now compared to then. I bring my requests before God, but they no longer dominate my prayer life. I do pray for others and seek wisdom from God in everyday matters. I also make time to hear from God.

Our needs very often drive our prayers to the extent we overlook two important aspects of prayer: praise and thanksgiving. We need to cultivate the habit of praising and worshiping him because he is worthy of our praise. We should give thanks for all God is doing and will do in our lives. Our prayers should focus on worship, praise, and thanksgiving. When I started to cultivate worship and praise in my prayer time, it was difficult; I didn't feel like it, but I did it anyway. I didn't stop until I was overcome with a deep sense of heartfelt meaning. In time, it became easier. I would remind myself about who God was, how great he was, and what he had done for me. With that perspective, it became easier to praise and worship him.

Thanksgiving came easy for me as I practiced this from early on in my walk with God. I am constantly overcome with gratitude when I think of the little things God does for me or when I sense his mercy and grace.

I thank God for all he has done in my life—the good, the bad, and the ugly. I am thankful that he held my hand and ushered me through my difficult times. "Don't worry about anything; instead, pray about everything. Tell God what you need, and thank him for all he has done" (Philippians 4:6).

Our hearts, souls, and minds benefit when we live in gratitude. We can learn much about thankfulness from David in the book of Psalms. Psalm 100 is about thanksgiving; a thankful heart is a joyful heart, and thankful people reap gladness.

Making Time

You have to make time for him or you will become a dry, needy Christian. Everything in life requires our time and attention, so we have to deliberately create time with him even if it's going to require making sacrifices. What are we willing to give up to make this very important appointment?

When I was self-employed, I could plan my day around my priorities. One was my time with God, and that would be in the morning, before I checked my emails or turned on my phone. Before I started working at the kindergarten, I was asked to come in and work for a while to make sure I liked the work. I started at eight and stayed until five; I ended up very tired and stressed. Then I still had to cook and do chores.

The next day, I took the matter up with God; I made it clear to him that I really wanted to work but felt it would make it tougher for me to meet my other obligations. He made me understand it was my choice. I don't have to work eight hours. I choose the hours I want to work so I can have time for the things I want to do. I was so relieved when this matter was resolved.

But again, I had another problem. There was no guarantee I would get the job, which is just ten minutes from our home. Again, I brought the matter before God; I told him it would be hard for me to spend two hours commuting to a job at which I worked only five hours a day. God was gracious; he provided the job down the road.

I decided in the beginning what was important for me—I worked fewer hours, but I was able to handle my other responsibilities to God, my family, recreation, and serving others.

> "Listen to my voice in the morning, Lord. Each morning I bring my requests to you and wait expectantly."
> —Psalm 5:3

Quiet Time

You can find quiet time for yourself many ways. Find the time and place that will work best for you. Jesus would go before daybreak to an isolated place to pray (Mark 1:35). We have many digital tools that can help us carve time out of our busy days. Most of the time, I would just read or listen to the Bible separate from my prayer time.

Bible reading or listening is important to me, so I do it every day. If I skip one day for any reason, I double my reading the next day. Get into the habit of reading the Bible and reflecting on it alone or with others. Prayerfully consider the implications this will have for your life; it's a time to enjoy his presence and hear from him. In *Touch the World through Prayer*, Wesley L. Duewel wrote, "God waits for you to communicate with him. You have an instant, direct access to God."

I have no set time for sharing with God. In the morning, I say a prayer for the day. If time allows, I walk to work and share intimate time with him. These prayers are often prompted by a hunger and a need to be with him. I pray spontaneously throughout the day as well. Practicing awareness of thought allows me to engage with God anytime.

Here's the prayer I say every morning.

Father, I thank you for this day. This is the day that the Lord has made; I will rejoice and be glad in it.

I give you my praise and honor for thou, Lord, are worthy to be praised and worshiped. Father, I exalt thee, I worship thee, I honor thee. Thou art worthy of praise and admiration. I magnify thy holy name. There is no one like you Lord. Glory and honor to you.

I give you thanks for your goodness and mercies toward me. I thank you for Jesus, who died for my sins. I thank you that I can have a personal relationship with you

I submit this day to you Lord, that you will bless this day, that it will be fruitful. Bless the work of my hands Lord. Create in me a clean heart and right spirit. And guard my heart, Lord. I pray that I may

be aware of my thoughts, feelings, and behavior. I
pray that I may be intentional in this day, making
a difference in the world around me. May I be a
light and vehicle of love, hope, and mercy unto the
world. Let me be a fragrance unto you. In Jesus's
name, amen.

Journaling

Journaling is therapeutic; it allows us to record our thoughts
and feelings. I find it a great tool as I can always go back and trace
my growth and progress. It is helpful in reflection and hearing from
God. I don't journal as often as I used to in the first seven years, but
it is still a vital part of my spiritual journey.

I journal my spiritual experiences, some prayers, and what I
hear from God. At one time, I wanted to burn all my journals, but
I realized how important that part of my spiritual history is playing
in my life today. That's where I was then and this is where I am
today. I still go back and read God's promises, his warnings, and his
reprimands he gave me throughout the years. I find a golden thread
of consistency running through my journals.

Journaling can also serve as a way to reflect; I pen important
events, lessons learned, and memorable moments and experiences
I can reread and reflect on. I also use my journal to write my goals
for the next year.

My birthday is in the middle of the year. I take time either a
day before or after to reflect on the six months gone by and to hear
from God about his plans for me for the next six months. Every
year, I go through my journals and reflect on my growth and my
goals achieved and goals not yet achieved.

Besides my personal writing to God in a journal, I also have
journals in which I write my thoughts on Bible verses. I also have a
journal in which I note the sermons I've heard and the books I've
read. I have kept them all.

Jim Rohn wrote this about journaling in a e-book, *How to Use a Journal:* "It is challenging to be a student of your own life, your own future, your own destiny. Don't trust your memory. When you listen to something valuable, write it down. When you come across something important, write it down. Take time to keep notes and to keep a journal."

> "They triumphed over him by the blood of the Lamb and by the word of their testimoney;"
> —Revelation 12:11 (NIV)

My Testimony

Revelation 12:11 (NIV) reads, "They triumphed over him by the blood of the Lamb and by the word of their testimony;" We overcame Satan though Jesus's death on the cross and by telling others all the good God has done in our lives. How will people learn what he has done for us if we don't tell them? Romans 10:17 says, "So faith comes from hearing, that, hearing the good news about Christ."

I love sharing my testimonies; they're my way of showing off who my God is. I often pray that God will protect what he has done in my life and that I will not forget the good work he has done in me.

When we forget, we stand the chance to take our faith, our growth, and our victories for granted. When we share our testimonies with others, their faith is stirred. The more we share our stories of faith, the more Satan is silenced. Don't take your small victories for granted; share them with the world and other believers. In Luke 8:39, Jesus told the man who was freed from demons to tell others what God had done for him.

The way we live is also a testimony to the world of what Jesus did for us on the cross. We may have changed hearts, but our actions have to line up with our words. Romans 8:19 (NIV): "For the creation waits in eager expectation for the children of God to be revealed." The world needs us to proclaim Jesus through our lives.

Matthew 5:16: "In the same way, let your light shine before others, so that they may see your good works and give glory to your Father who is in heaven."

Community

I cannot imagine my life without the body of Christ. Wherever we moved, the first thing we did was find a church.

You cannot grow by yourself. You need a place where you and like-minded people can grow in faith. You can argue that you don't need other people to grow, that you can read the Bible by yourself, listen to gospel music, and listen to sermons online. This attitude of isolation is deadly for any believer. There is no safety or growth in isolation. We were not created to live in isolation; we were created to be connected and to connect with others.

> "Therefore, accept each other just as Christ has accepted you so that God will be given glory."
> —Romans 15:7

We all need a place where we belong, a place to love and be loved, a place where we can share our personal resources. God wants us to live in community. Yes, we might be offended or offend others, and we will face disappointment in others or disappoint them. But God accepts us all in spite of our flaws. Romans 15:7 tells us to accept each other as Christ accepted us. The fellowship we share with each other consists of what Jesus did for us. We are bound together as brothers and sisters in Christ. We can find safety in this environment and be ourselves. We can receive and give encouragement week after week. We need others to watch out for us, minister to us, and correct us. We need to work with each other to build his kingdom.

So now you Gentiles are no longer strangers and foreigners. You are citizens along with all of God's holy people. You are members of God's family.

Together we are his house, built on the foundation of
the apostles and the prophets. And the cornerstone
is Christ Jesus himself. (Ephesians 2:19–20)

We are a family growing, learning, serving together, and living
the very heart and nature of heaven. As a family, we should fight
every attempt to bring division among us. We are committed to
the universal vision of the body to grow the kingdom of God and
create a safe environment for newcomers to discover it. When we
come together on a Sunday, we shape and create an atmosphere in
our hearts for change and for those who are seeking and hungry
for hope.

We are the body of Christ, and Christ is the head of the church
(Colossians 1:24). When we come together as the body, we celebrate
and go out into the world as representatives of his body. We are
lights to the world and represent the body of Christ to the world.

Many churches offer home groups, small groups, or life groups
that meet during the week. I love the name *life groups*; that says it
all. I call small groups the heartbeat of church where community
really happens. Hebrews 10:24–25 tells us, "Let us think of ways to
motivate one another to acts of love and good works. And let us not
neglect our meeting together, as some people do, but encourage one
another." Believers come together, authentically share God's Word,
and pray and care for each other. Special and lifelong friendship
circles are formed through life groups, which can become life
supports for many. Instant prayer chains are formed when the need
arises. I am still connected to my life group of five years ago. In
her book, *Daring Greatly*, Brene Brown said, "Connection is why we
are here. We are hardwired to connect with others. It's what gives
purpose and meaning to our lives."

Chapter 11

Matters of the Heart

> If you are distressed by anything external, the pain is
> not due to the thing itself, but to your estimate of it and
> thus you have power to revoke it at any moment.
> —Marcus Aurelius

Trials

Of course we will face trials in our lives. When things go wrong,
we need to be assured God is still on the throne and in control. We
stay in the shelter of the Most High and find rest in him (Psalm 91).
Life will throw curveballs at us, but our attitude about them will
determine the outcome.

> Dear brothers and sisters, when troubles of any
> kind come your way, consider it an opportunity
> for great joy. For you know that when your faith is
> tested, your endurance has a chance to grow. So let
> it grow, for when your endurance is fully developed,
> you will be perfect and complete, needing nothing.
> (James 1:2–4)

When we find ourselves being shaken, that means God is testing us and preparing us for the next stage in our lives. We are never alone during testing and trying times. When we are locked in God's security system, we will never be caught off guard by tests; we will be ready to face our challenges.

A great example of this is the story of Joseph, who was sold as a slave by his envious brothers. He was working for Potiphar as a supervisor in his household. Joseph made great progress in his work and was promoted. Potiphar's wife tried to seduce him, but he refused to give in to her demands. He was subsequently accused of attempted rape and was thrown in jail. Joseph had two dreams (Genesis 37:5–11) about ruling over his brothers. He went through several years of hardship but kept his heart in the right place and remained faithful to God.

God was with Joseph, and he later showed mercy and forgiveness toward his brothers. Genesis 45:5: "But don't be upset, and don't be angry with yourselves for selling me to this place. It was God who sent me here ahead of you to preserve your lives." Just imagine if Joseph's heart had been full of bitterness. The story and the history of the Israelites would have taken another turn.

> "But don't be upset, and don't be angry with yourselves for selling me to this place. It was God who sent me here ahead of you to preserve your lives."
> —Genesis 45:5

How you handle your trials is up to you. If you choose to trust in yourself or someone else to resolve your troubles, you will come up short. Trusting God with your troubles will result in joy and peace; you will know he will work all things for the good. Why burden yourself when God can take care of all your worries? Over the years, I have faced many troubles and so often resolved to take matters into my own hands, but that resulted in more worry and anxiety.

Deep inside, we know we cannot trust ourselves to solve our issues, but through impatience and egoism, we burden ourselves;

we think God is too busy or will take too long to resolve a matter. I have now disciplined myself to immediately cast my burden on him. I am awed every time I give my problems to God by the sense of peace and assurance I gain. I detach myself from an issue and wait for him to act on my behalf. I know I can trust him. As I am writing this, our family is facing a couple of tests, but again, I choose to trust God. I do not know the reason or outcome of this situation, but I know God will handle it perfectly.

We will face storms in life but can rest assured Jesus is with us. This can be challenging; when the disciples faced a storm and were fearful, Jesus reprimanded them for having little faith (Matthew 8:23–27). They had focused on the problem—the storm—instead of on the solution—Jesus, who was with them. We tend to react as the disciples did. Jesus is with us always, so we can rest assured he will calm the storms in our lives even if they seem overwhelming. We are to stand firm in our faith (1 Corinthians 16:13), knowing who we are in Christ Jesus and waiting for the calm he will bring. We are to hold onto only him, our anchor in all our storms. His grace is made perfect in our weakness. Romans 15:13 tells us, "I pray that God, the source of hope, will fill you completely with joy and peace because you trust in him. Then you will overflow with confident hope through the power of the Holy Spirit." We will experience joy, peace, and hope when we stay focused on him. We must trust him even when our hearts grow faint and weary and we want to give in to fear and worry. We must remind ourselves of God's goodness and faithfulness.

My Story

What I had prayed for years not to happen did happen in January 2009. During our financial difficulty, I had one prayer—that God would not let my brother or my dad die because we wouldn't have been able to handle the funeral expenses. My brother had been ill since 2004, and my father was suffering from dementia. At the end of December 2008, I prayed to God to help me give up on my business, to let it go, as there seemed to be no signs things would get better with it.

When he was dying, my brother asked me to come to Namibia to be at his side, but I couldn't afford the trip. My family offered to pay, but I declined their help; it was a matter between God and me, and I trusted God to act in his nature. My brother died on a Tuesday. The funeral was to take place on Saturday. Though I had no money, I trusted I'd be able to fly out on Thursday and attend the memorial service that night.

On Thursday morning, money came into our account that enabled us to pay our employees, our outstanding rent, and my ticket to Namibia. I could go in peace knowing my affairs were in order. Though I didn't get to say good-bye to my brother, I chose to cherish the times I had visited him and the many phone calls he made to me to talk. I cherished the times I took care of him when he was with me. On the day I helped him check into the rehabilitation center, I shared his most fearful moments. That was all okay with me. He and his family had visited us in December; I knew it was his last visit. My dad died that same year.

I wasn't angry with God. I talked matters through with him and settled them. I miss my brother and cry when I tell his story. The loss of my dad was different; he had suffered from dementia for a long time; I had said good-bye to him long before he died. It's sad to see your loved ones in a helpless state. My dad was a special person.

Trust

Everything in our lives is about relationship. Where there is relationship, there has to be trust. All relationships are grounded in trust. As I mentioned earlier, I had trust issues in the beginning of my walk, but God restored my trust in others by blessing me with two great friends and the ability to trust people for who they were. I learned to share my burdens with others without feeling insecure or threatened. What they would do with my story was their problem. My attitude was that the more people who know about my problem, the lighter my burden would become. To be trusting is not a sign of weakness. Some people will try to take advantage of our trust, but Psalm 146:3 warns us, "Don't put your confidence in powerful people; there is no help for you there."

We have no control over others' actions, but we can control how we deal with them. We all have had issues with others who broke trust with us. We can get angry with that, but we can and should forgive them and move on. This can be hard, but it is always in our best interests to forgive.

Marriages are a different ball game, right? Lack of trust in a marriage is always tough to deal with. But it's a matter of the heart. Trust and forgiveness go hand in hand. There must be a willingness to forgive for trust to be restored. It's not easy to forgive, but it's a choice we have to make so we can remain in right standing with God.

> "Such love has no fear, because perfect love expels all fear."
> —1 John 4:18

Unforgiveness is a sin; we need to forgive others so God can forgive us. Trust is the cornerstone of any relationship. Some think that others have to earn their trust by constantly proving themselves when in fact both parties have to work at creating loving, healthy, and trusting relationships. We trust God because we learn about his love, character, heart, and plans for us through his Word; trust begins and ends with God. We allow God to work in us so we can trust others or have our trust restored. We learn from scripture that love is not self-seeking; it doesn't keep records. I have experienced this; when trust was broken, I forgave, and almost immediately, God restored that trust.

When we break trust, we should take responsibility and rightfully admit we have committed an offense. We should be humble and confess our sin to another so God can forgive us. Be sincere in a way that the other person also feels validated in the process.

Walking in Forgiveness

When we accept God's forgiveness, we forgive ourselves, and so must we forgive others. Matthew 6:12 is clear about this: "Forgive us our sins, as we have forgiven those who sin against us." But many believers live in unforgiveness; they aren't willing to pardon others for the wrongs they have inflicted on them. This is a sin. They live lives bound up and are not aware of it. Unforgiveness causes sickness and disease. The easiest way we can heal ourselves is to forgive. Forgiveness is our most powerful tool; we can use it to live in wholeness. Mark 11:25 tells us, "When you are praying, first forgive anyone you are holding a grudge against, so that your Father in heaven will forgive your sins, too."

Forgiveness is a choice, an act of our will. Forgiving others is our gift to ourselves, and others may even benefit from it. Forgiveness doesn't require our condoning the offenses committed against us, but unforgiveness compounds the offense. The longer we walk in unforgiveness, the harder it becomes for us to forgive. It causes hatred, bitterness, rebellion, anger, strife, and disunity, while forgiveness produces unity, harmony, and peace.

We have to be mindful about it if we want to live in forgiveness. We cannot ignore our sins or consider them too small to worry about. Some think they don't have to tell their spouses everything. That's the same as saying what happens in Vegas stays in Vegas. It's wrong to be burdened by an unconfessed sin. It can cause you to shun God in fear. The longer you hold onto it, the bigger it gets, and the consequences can be far- reaching. When we sin, someone always bears the consequences for it; somebody is picking up the tab for the action.

> "Finally, I confessed all my sins to you and stopped trying to hide my guilt. I said to myself, 'I will confess my rebellion to the Lord.' And you forgave me! All my guilt was gone."
> —Psalm 32:5

Oh, what joy for those whose disobedience is forgiven, whose sin is put out of sight! Yes, what joy for those whose record the Lord has cleared of guilt, whose lives are lived in complete honesty! When I refused to confess my sin, my body wasted away, and I groaned all day long. Day and night your hand of discipline was heavy on me. My strength evaporated like water in the summer heat. Finally, I confessed all my sins to you and stopped trying to hide my guilt. I said to myself, "I will confess my rebellion to the Lord." And you forgave me! All my guilt was gone. (Psalm 32:1–5)

We are to walk uprightly before God with clean hearts and live in right standing with him. One bit of undealt sin and forgiveness is an open door for Satan to lodge an attack and lay a charge against us.

Fear

There are all kinds of fear, but fear of the Lord is a good fear. Judges 6 contains the story of Gideon. When the Lord told him strike down the Midianites, Gideon wondered why God wanted to send him and his tiny tribe to fight a mighty people. He wondered how the Lord would be with them when they were all but destroyed. God had to give Gideon a sign to confirm his favor on him.

Later, when God instructed him to tear down Baal's altar and cut down the Asherah poles, he was afraid for his family. He did it at night rather than during the day. When the people discovered Gideon had removed their shrines, they wanted to kill him. God allowed this doubtful, fearful man with limited gifts to win the battle. Gideon was obedient, and that was to his credit. Sometimes, it's okay to be fearful as long as we do what God expects us to do.

Fear is a threat to us believers; we need to know what it looks like, identify it immediately, confront it, and rebuke it. As I wrote earlier, fear was a huge factor in my life in a few areas. I have to remind myself constantly that I'm not afraid, that I have the spirit that raised Jesus from the dead in me, that I have authority over the enemy. Fear breeds worry and anxiety, and worry and anxiety breed more fear. Fear is the enemy of faith. The enemy is a master at creating and sowing thoughts of fear. If we are not vigilant, he will devour us. "Give all your worries and cares to God for he cares about you. Stay alert! Watch out for your great enemy, the devil. He prowls around like a roaring lion, looking for someone to devour" (1 Peter 5:7–8).

> "Stay alert! Watch out for your great enemy, the devil. He prowls around like a roaring lion, looking for someone to devour."
> —1 Peter 5:8

How often do we take matters into own hands when we're trying to solve a crisis and make unwise decisions instead of trusting God to take care of matters? When we try to resolve our problems instead of relying on him, it very often backfires on us. We become impatient and run ahead of him rather than waiting on him. We rely on our strength instead of God's. We create unfavorable and uncertain circumstances that result in panic and fear, and that stops us from living in Christ's fullness.

Fear creates doubt, confusion, insecurity, lack of trust, instability, panic, suspicion, cowardice, apprehension, depression, and fright among many other negatives. Fear's physical symptoms include irregular heart rates, indigestion, sweating, shortness of breath, restlessness, and insomnia to mention just a few problems. Fear results in stress, and that can have a detrimental effect on our mental and physical well-being.

Fear takes place in the mind, a battlefield. We are to live with a sound mind, and we can do that if we are aware of the thoughts we allow into our minds. Isaiah 41:10 says, "Don't be afraid, for I am with you. Don't be discouraged for I am your God. I will strengthen you and help you. I will hold you up with my victorious right hand."

We can fight back with the Word of God, our powerful weapon, breaking down strongholds. Psalm 27:1 tells us, "The Lord is my light and my salvation—so why should I be afraid. The Lord is my fortress, protecting me from danger, so why should I tremble?" Even in uncertain times, we should trust God and put our total dependence in him. Our future is in his hands, and when he leads us, he will provide and sustain us.

Sin

Sin is an immoral act, a transgression against divine law. To sin is to miss the mark of God's expectations. Sin separates us from God. In his book *Celebration of Discipline*, Richard Foster referred to sin as the slavery of ingrained habits, and there is no slavery that can compare to the slavery of ingrained habits of sin (see Romans 7:5). We are to free ourselves of ingrained, sinful habits.

We should also guard against becoming insensitive to sin; we run the risk of not being able to discern right from wrong. In Galatians 5:13, we read, "We have been called to live in freedom, my brothers and sister. But don't use your freedom to satisfy your sinful nature." And 1 Corinthians 10 deals with the effects of sin on Israel. Paul instructed us in verses 6–7,

> These things happened as a warning to us, so that we would not crave evil things as they did, or worship idols as they did. Verse 10-11 And don't grumble as some of them did, and then were destroyed by the angel of death. These things happened to them as examples for us. They were written down to warn us who live as the end of age.

Though we have this warning, the church of today is struggling the same way it did back then.

Titus 3:4 tells us, "When the kindness and love of God our

savior appeared, he saved us, not because of righteous things we had done, but because of his mercy." When we are gripped by his grace, we will want to do what is right and pleasing.

Jesus faced temptation, but he had knowledge of who he was through the Word. He knew he had the authority and power of the Holy Spirit and overcame the devil.

> God blesses those who patiently endure testing and temptation. Afterward they will receive the crown of life that has promised to those who love him. And remember when you are being tempted, do not say, "God is tempting me." God is never tempted to do wrong, and he never tempts anyone else. Temptation comes from our own desires, which entice us and drag us away. These desires give birth to sinful actions. And when sin is allowed to grow, it gives birth to death. (James 1:12-15)

What we occupy our minds with will result in action. The more we entertain fleshly thoughts, the more likely we are to act on them. That's when we respond by saying we have been tempted. When we fail to take action after one wrong thought, the next follows quickly, and this can result in spiritual death. We become insensitive to sin and no longer feel remorse.

Sin affects our relationship with God; we hide from him. Sin is never neutral or private; others are often affected by our sin. But the Word of God is our weapon against the enemy. The closer we are to God, the more aware we are of sin. Psalm 139:23 says, "Search me, O God and know my heart; test me and know my anxious thoughts. Point out

> "Search me, O God and know my heart; test me and know my anxious thoughts. Point out anything in me that offends you, and lead me along the path of everlasting life."
> —Psalm 139:23-24

anything in me that offends you, and lead me along the path of everlasting life."

Faith

Faith is believing in something we have no visible or physical proof of. Faith is based solely on trust. Our faith is manifested through our trust in God. We believe God spoke the world into existence because of what we read in the Bible. Hebrews 11 is a compilation of great stories about faith; it bears witness to the depth to which certain people mentioned in the chapter trusted God. Hebrews 11:1 tells us, "Now faith is being sure of what we hope for and certain of what we do not see." Faith and hope go together; we cannot have hope and not faith. We will hope for whatever we have faith in.

We present our requests to God in the hope and trust that he will grant them. When God responds, our faith is stirred. So the next time we come to God, we have even greater hope, trust and faith that he will respond to our prayers. And so we grow in faith.

When I bring my requests to God, I intentionally remember all my answered prayers and victories. That heightens my faith and hope that God will come through for me. Should my prayers not be answered in the way I expected them to be, I am still hopeful and thankful that God knows best and that he acts on my behalf. When we act in faith on the knowledge of who God is, he will reward us. In Hebrews 11:6, we learn it is impossible to please God without faith. Anyone who wants to come to him must believe he exists and rewards those who sincerely seek him.

Abraham, referred to as the father of our faith, is one of the greatest examples of faith in the Bible. Genesis 12–25 tells us of the tests he underwent; he obeyed and believed in God, and it counted for him in such a great way that he made it to the hall of fame in the Bible.

Romans 10:17 says, "Faith comes by hearing, that is hearing the

Good News about Christ." We cannot grow our faith if we don't know anything about God and his Word. If we want to develop six-packs, we cannot stop after one workout; we have to train almost every day to shape those muscles. So is it with faith; we have to exercise it all the time if we want to develop unwavering faith muscles,

> "Faith comes by hearing, that is hearing the Good News about Christ."
> —Romans 10:17

which is harder than developing our physical muscles. It will take sweat and tears, but it will be so worth it.

We need patience as we wait for our muscles to take shape. At times, we'll have to wait for God to respond or act on our behalf. When we stop exercising, our six-packs will disappear with time. We should guard against complacency or settling for a comfort zone in which we could become dull in our faith.

In *The Attitude of Faith*, Frank Damazio wrote,

> Faith is nurtured by the proper functioning of the mind. The spirit of faith is assimilated into the mind and merged with the word of God residing in the mind, creating a chemistry of growing faith. Begin today to discipline your mind in right thinking—thinking that is in agreement with the word of God.

Obedience

An abundant life is grounded in obedience to God; we must listen to him and act on what he requires of us. This idea is being taken lightly in the church today, even by me. I find myself asking, *What does God want from me?* But not too long ago, someone gave me the Word: "I never told you to be careful but to be obedient." At first, I thought, *What?* But the Holy Spirit immediately reminded me, and I knew exactly what he was talking about—something God told me in 2014.

Here's a famous verse in 1 Samuel 15:22: "Samuel replied, 'what is more pleasing to the Lord: your burnt offerings and sacrifices or your obedience to his voice? Listen! Obedience is better than sacrifice and submission is better than offering the fat of rams.'" King Saul had gone to battle and spared the life of the Amalekite king Agag, but he took all the plunder he could in spite of what God had told him to do. When Samuel confronted him, he argued that he had obeyed the Lord, that he had destroyed the Amalekites and had taken the best of the cattle and sheep to sacrifice them to the Lord. God wasn't impressed. Saul later confessed he had sinned and had given into the pressures of his men. Through this act of disobedience, Saul lost his dynasty to David.

God is always speaking to us through his Word or someone else. We should create a time, place, and environment in our hearts to listen to him. Hebrews 12:25 reminds us, "Be careful that you do not refuse to listen to the One who is speaking."

Serving

Part of our growth requires us to offer our service to God. To serve is an act of worship. An expression of love is fellowship—sharing ourselves with others by giving our time and sharing our gifts with them. Jesus's whole life was about serving others; everything he did reflected a servant heart. Matthew 20:26 reads, "Whoever wants to be a leader among you must be your servant." Matthew 20:28 tells us, "For even the son of came not be served but to serve others and to give his life as a ransom for many." Greatness in God's kingdom can be achieved only by serving others. We all can and should serve

> "God has given each of you a gift from his great variety of spiritual gifts. Use them well to serve one another."
> — 1 Peter 4:10

in some way or another. No matter where we are in our journeys, we can offer something meaningful to others. We learn in 1 Peter 4:10 that God has given each of us a gift from his great variety of spiritual gifts; we should use them to serve one another.

In my most trying of times, I have found serving to be the right antidote for and a kind of escape from my troubles. Putting others' needs before my own is uplifting and has always left me with a special kind of thankfulness.

We must also keep in mind that when serving, we serve each other and our leaders. By serving in the local church, we are signaling to the leaders that we stand with them, that we are aligning ourselves with their vision, and that we commit to build the kingdom of God with them. An important characteristic to display and to cultivate when serving is faithfulness. Be there when you agree to serve. After all, we are serving God, and he deserves our faithfulness. Serve with excellence as if you were being paid to do it.

Chapter 12

Love

> Since love grows within you, so beauty grows.
> For love is the beauty of the soul.
> —St. Augustine

In 1 John 4:18, we read, "There is no fear in love but perfect love drives out fear." Love and fear cannot coexist. Love is positive; fear is negative. When we operate in a love mode, there won't be a place for fear or negativity. We will be positive in heart, mind, soul, and strength and not express any hostility toward God. Romans 8:7 tells us the sinful nature is always hostile to God. We are to follow the Holy Spirit, who is in us to guide our thinking, feeling, and behaving.

> And you must love the Lord your God with all
> your heart, all your soul, all your mind and your
> strength. The second is equally important: Love
> your neighbor as yourself. No other commandment
> is greater than these. (Mark 12:30)

This commandment is like three strands beautifully woven together to form a thick, strong strand resulting in the greatest love. These three have to be in alignment. You cannot have one without the other. Love is the greatest and highest gift, and we are to live this kind of love every day in every way. Everything we have—our talents, gifts, riches, wisdom, knowledge—is little in comparison to love.

> If I could speak all the languages of earth and of angles, but didn't love others, I would only be a noisy gong or a clanging cymbal. If I had the gift of prophecy, and if I understood all of Gods secret plans and possessed all knowledge, and if I had faith that I could move mountains, but didn't lover others, I would be nothing. If I gave everything I have to the poor and even sacrificed my body, I could boast about it, but if I didn't love others, I would have gained nothing. Love is patient and kind. Love is not jealous or boastful or proud or rude. It does not demand its own way. It is not irritable, and it keeps no record of being wronged. It does not rejoice about injustice but rejoices whenever the truth wins out. Love never gives up, never loses faith, is always hopeful, and endures through every circumstance. Prophecy and speaking in unknown languages and special knowledge will become useless. But love will last forever! Three things will last forever—faith, hope and love—and the greatest of these is love. (1 Corinthians 13:1–13)

> "Three things will last forever—faith, hope and love—and the greatest of these is love."
> —1 Corinthians 13:13

Love God

The nature of God is love. We were created to love God. Everything was created because of his love for us, his ultimate creation. Love was and still is the motive for creation. Because of his love for us, he longs for us to experience his love. Love is to be our driving force. We should love him with all our heart, soul, mind, and strength. Our hearts are to be moved by love, our thoughts are to be love inspired, and our actions are to be of love. We are to breathe love; it should flow through our veins at all times. We are to constantly breed love.

We love God because he first loved us. We love him because he has bestowed on us such a great gift through Jesus, who died for our sins. We love him because we have his Spirit in us. We love him because of his kindness toward us. We love him because of his goodness and favor toward us. There is no end to the many reasons why we should love God. The footprints of his love are on every page of the Bible.

Love Self

This is the hardest thing for many of us to. What we believe about ourselves affects our lives and those of others. Through accepting ourselves, we are able to love ourselves. If we do not love ourselves, we cannot love God and others. Through loving ourselves and accepting ourselves for whom and what God made us to be, we are thanking God for the gift of life he gave us. Ephesians 1:5: "God decided in advance to adopt us into his own family by bringing us to himself through Jesus Christ." He handpicked each one of us for his kingdom.

Loving ourselves requires our acceptance of everything about ourselves—our height, weight, looks, and so on. By accepting ourselves for who God made us to be, we acknowledge that our past has been nailed to the cross and are thankful to God for saving us and allowing us a new identity in Christ. By accepting ourselves, we are saying we take responsibility for our

> "May the Lord make your love for one another and for all people grow and overflow, just as our love for you overflows."
> —1 Thessalonians 3:12

spiritual, emotional, and physical well-being. Christ has accepted us; we believe that based on his Word. God sees us as perfect creations, his sons and daughters, and we should see ourselves the same way. We are forgiven and are new creations with new identities.

Love Others

In 1 Thessalonians 3:12, we read, "May the Lord make your love for one another and for all people grow and overflow, just as our love for you overflows." It's difficult to love our neighbors day in day out, but God requires that. I have to remind myself every day when I find myself surrounded by people and doing everyday things such as riding a bus, walking in the park, or shopping that God loves others just as much as he loves me. With so many bad things happening every day in the world, it becomes harder and harder to exercise this commandment. Rick Warren wrote in *The Purpose Driven Life*: "Learning to love unselfishly is not an easy task. It runs counter to our self-centered nature." There is more hate than love in the world. We are daily confronted by the hate in the world when we watch the news. We have to do more than just tolerate our neighbors; we have to love them. Love thinks no evil; it fosters no hate toward others. Read 1 Corinthians 13.

We can't wait until we feel love for others; that could take a very long time. Love is a choice. Love is an action. Giving someone a warm smile is an act of love. Offering to carry someone's bag is an act of love. Giving up our seat on the bus to an elderly person is an act of love. Offering to listen to a lonely person is an act of love.

Love has many faces. When we, the church, get this whole message of who we are in Christ Jesus right, we will begin to live love, be the love, and extend the love to a world in need of seeing and experiencing Christ in us. We are the hope the world needs; it's time for us to take our rightful places in the world. We have hidden too long behind the curtain of misunderstanding the work of the cross. Church, we are free, we are forgiven, we are healed, and we are new creations. I love Romans 5:5: "We know how dearly God loves us, because he has given us the Holy Spirit to fill our heart with his love." Our hearts are filled with love. We have no excuse. We need to act out of this love every day in every way.

Chapter 13

Living the Abundant Life

To be utterly content and grateful with all of life is to enjoy the fullness of life.

John 10:10 reads, "The thief comes only to steal, slaughter, and destroy. I have come to that they may have life, and have it abundantly." This verse has various meanings for various people. For me, it means I should enjoy the fullness of life in all areas of my life in my body, soul, and spirit. I am to know who I am in Christ Jesus and live in wholeness. My identity is in Christ. I should foster healthy relationships with my family, friends, and others and be content with my material position. Regardless of where I may find myself in life, I will enjoy the abundance of life.

Four years ago after a long period of difficulty, I decided this is where I would position myself: to live the last part of that verse—living the abundant life instead of just living. I have claimed Jeremiah 17:8 for myself: "I will be like a tree planted along a riverbank, with roots that reach deep into the water. I am a tree not bothered by the heat or worried by long months of drought. My leaves stay green, and I never stop producing fruit." I have roots deep in the water, and my leaves stay green during my trying times. At times, I grow weary, but I never surrender to failure or hopelessness.

We can claim and live out so many verses in the Bible, which has no shortage of truth, promise, and encouragement. Ephesians 3:20: "Now all glory to God, who is able, through his mighty power at work within us, to accomplish infinitely more than we might ask or think." We believers have the great advantage that his spirit is in us. When we stay plugged into him, his spirit, he can do abundantly and above our wildest imaginations more things in, for, and through us.

> "Now all glory to God, who is able, through his mighty power at work within us, to accomplish infinitely more than we might ask or think."
> —Ephesians 3:20

John 10:27–28 tells us, "My sheep listen to my voice; I know them, and they follow me. I give them eternal life, and they never perish. No one can snatch them away from me." As followers of Christ, we have the assurance that Satan cannot harm us or pluck us out of God's hand.

To live the abundant life, we have to continually grow spiritually and intellectually. Discovering new heights and living our purpose will enrich our lives and those of others.

Characteristics of an Abundant Person

Philippians 4:12 says, "I know how to live on almost nothing or with everything. I have learned the secret of living in every situation, whether it is with a full stomach or empty, with plenty or little." Paul was writing about the secret to living—being content regardless of our circumstances.

Abundant people live intentionally every day. They are confident of and secure in their identity. They always seek ways to add value to others. They are people of significance with a servant heart. They are large-capacity people who can stretch like a rubber band. They share their resources whether they have plenty or little. They live out of the conviction of their hearts. They are courageous and bold, and they are messengers of hope.

To not embrace our identity we have in Christ will cause us

to miss the privileges, blessings, and the abundance God offers us. I have much to experience in my place of abundance; I'm only beginning to live and taste it, and I'm eager to know and grow in this area that Christ wants me to have and enjoy. I invite you to embark with me and others on the most fulfilling journey we will ever take as we strive to live in a way that pleases him.

When we started going through the severe financial crisis in 2008, I scrapped all my goals and decided to have just one—to live a life that was pleasing to God. That was my only goal for four years. I have started to make goal lists again, but that one remains at the top of my list. When we get this right, we move in the right direction of experiencing and living an abundant life.

I have put a few words together to remind us to stay in a place of growing and experiencing the abundant of life daily.

- **Reflect** daily on what is in your heart—what you are feeling and thinking.
- **Refrain** from entertaining destructive thoughts and from having unhealthy conversations.
- **Refuse** to believe the lies of the enemy. He is the initiator of bad and negative thoughts.
- **Release** every negative thought and behavior.
- **Redirect** your thoughts to what is true and good.
- **Remind** yourself of God's promises for your life and Bible verses to fight against evil.
- **Remain** in the vine. Stay connected and in communion with him and other believers.

1 Timothy 4:10 reads, "To this end we toil and strive, because we have our hope set on the living God, who is the savior of all people, especially of those who believe." As we go through this life and regardless of what we may endure, our hope remains in him. We hold onto this hope because we know we are his chosen people and should strive therefore for the eternal crown we will receive.

Appendix

Questions for Reflection

Part 1
Chapter 1
Who Am I?

Can you say yes to the following statements?

- I am loved by God.
- I am accepted by God.
- I am a new creation.
- My identity is fully galvanized in Christ Jesus.

If your answers are no, what is the reason?

Say aloud, "I am loved by God." As you say this, feel the emotion of his love toward you.

Say aloud, "I am accepted and chosen by God." Do the same as suggested above.

Say aloud, "I am forgiven by God." Do the same as suggested above.

Say aloud, "All my sins have been forgiven. I have been made righteous." Do as per above.

Repeat this exercise for thirty days. Read Psalm 139, and for thirty days, meditate on these statements throughout the day. Say them aloud if you want.

Pick a verse in Psalm 139 that speaks to you personally and meditate on it. Make it your own.

If you haven't tried journaling yet, get any kind of blank book and start penning your heart and thoughts to God.

Chapter 2
I Am Loved by God

For God so loved the world that he gave his one and only son, so that whoever believes in him shall not perish but have eternal life.
—John 3:16 (NIV)

Can you relate to the love of God for you? Express your thoughts and feelings on whether you can or cannot.

What is still holding you back from experiencing his love for you?

I have loved you with an everlasting love, I
have drawn you with unfailing kindness
—Jeremiah 31:3

How do feel reading this verse? Memorize it.

Chapter 3
I Am Accepted and Chosen by God

All those the father gives me will come to me, and
whoever comes to me I will never drive away.
—John 6:37 NIV

Do you feel accepted by God? If not, what might be the reason?

Do you feel you have to prove yourself to God?

If you would change your view about this, what would need to change?

> Those the Father has given me will come to me,
> and I will never reject them. —John 6:37

> You have been chosen to be a child of God. What
> is your understanding of this verse?

Chapter 4
I Have Been Forgiven by God

> In him we have redemption through this blood, the forgiveness
> of sins, in accordance with the riches of God's grace.
> —Ephesians 1:7

Do you live everyday out of the conviction that all your sins have been forgiven? If not, what are you uncertain about? Are you able to tell God this?

What could the consequences be on your spiritual journey should you not settle this matter?

What steps should you take to resolve this? Can you take them now?

I—yes, I alone will blot your sins for my own sake
and will never think of them again.—Isaiah 43:25

Are you now able to accept that all your sins are
forgiven?

Chapter 5
I Am a New Creation

This means that anyone who belongs to Christ has become
a new person. The old life is gone; a new life has begun.
—2 Corinthians 5:17

How do you feel about this verse? Can you completely embrace
this truth? If not, why not?

What exactly do you struggle with? What are you wrestling with
to let go of?

You have the opportunity to bring those before God now.
Here's a prayer you can say: "Father, I accept that Jesus died for
all of my sins, and that his blood was shed for all of my pain and
sickness. I choose now to release and surrender [mention here what
you wish to release] at the foot of the cross. I pray right now that
you bring healing and restoration to my heart and my life. I thank
you for the healing and restoration I receive now in Jesus's name."

God is fully aware of where you are right now. You're not alone.
Embrace his presence right now.

You have taken account of my wanderings, put
my tears in your bottle and are they not in your
book.—Psalm 56:8

We know that God causes everything to work
together for the good of those who love God and
are called according to his purpose for them.—
Romans 8:28

How do you feel about this verse? What does it
mean to you right now?

Part 2
Chapter 6
Renewing Your Mind

Don't copy the behavior and customs of this world, but let God
transform you into a new person by changing the way you think.
—Romans 12:2

What is your response to this verse? Do you find it hard to
carry out?

Do you have daily time to read and pray? If not, what's keeping
you from doing that?

If you don't make time, you will have trouble renewing your
mind and throwing off your old life. What will it take to readjust
your life?

Chapter 7
How Does the Mind Work?

So letting your sinful nature control your mind leads to death.
But letting the spirit control your mind leads to life and peace.
—Romans 8:6

In what condition is your mind? Is it a well-cultivated garden, or is it overgrown with weeds?

What beliefs and habits have you grown up with that aren't in line with God's truth? How did they come about? Parents? Culture? Environment?

Can you recognize a connection between your behavior and your emotional conditioning? Elaborate on how your experiences have shaped you.

How did these have an impact on your life?

What types of situations really aggravate you?

Can you be totally open and honest to God about how you're feeling?

Is there an area you need to bring before God? Do that now.

What new beliefs/habits do you wish to instill? How will you implement them?

Are you ready to invest the time required to change your false beliefs and habits?

Chapter 8
Thoughts

> We demolish arguments and every pretension that sets
> itself up against the knowledge of God, and we take
> captive every thought to make it obedient to Christ.
> —2 Corinthians 10:5 NIV

List the thoughts that frequently occupy your mind.

How much of it is destructive?

What actions are you taking to replace your bad thoughts?

What are your thoughts about yourself?

Find promises in the Bible on God's view about you. How is this truth helping you change the way you think and feel about yourself?

> Fix your thoughts on what is true, and honorable, and
> right, and pure, and lovely, and admirable. Think about
> things that are excellent and worthy of praise.
> —Philippians 4:8

What do you think led Paul to give us such a tall instruction?

How would your life improve if you managed your thoughts and feelings better?

Select key verses to help you in this process. I have intentionally written out scriptures for you to have at hand, but pick out your own as well.

Chapter 9
Practicing Awareness

> For we are not fighting against flesh and blood enemies,
> but against evil rulers and authorities of the unseen
> world, against mighty powers in this dark world,
> and against evil spirits in the heavenly places.
> —Ephesians 6:12

Can you sense your feelings when you get up in the morning? What kind of feelings are they?

Were you able to determine their origin? What were you thinking about?

Were you able to resolve them? Bring them before God. Share your thoughts and feelings with him. Ask for his peace over the matter.

> You will keep in perfect peace whose mind is fixed on you.
> —Isaiah 26:3

Can you cultivate a habit of awareness of your thoughts throughout the day? How could you do this?

Part 3
Chapter 10
Growing in Him

> Let your roots grow down into him, and let your lives be
> built on him. Then your faith will grow strong in the truth
> you were taught, and you will overflow with thankfulness.
> —Colossians 2:7

How are you doing in reading your Bible? What do you need to do to make that part of your day?

Are you able to apply biblical truths to your life? If not, share you reasons.

Could your response be connected to a false belief system?

Are you able to make time in the day to pray? If not, what is the reason?

What needs to change so you can come to him?

What would be the benefit if you did so every day or even more often?

Are you part of a local church? If not, what's keeping you from becoming one? Is this helpful to your spiritual growth?

What other form of community do you have? Do you belong to a life group or house group?

In which way do you contribute to community life?

If you served a church, in what capacity would that be?

Take the steps necessary to engage and commit to a local church.

God has given me the responsibility of serving his church by proclaiming his entire message to you.
—Colossians 1:25

Chapter 11
Matters of the Heart

Dear brothers and sisters, when troubles of any kind come your way, consider it an opportunity for great joy. For you know that when your faith is tested, your endurance has a chance to grow. So let it grow, for when your endurance is fully developed, you will be perfect and complete, needing nothing.
—James 1:2–4

What is your response to this verse?

How do you deal with the curveballs life throws at you? Who do you run to first?

Can you completely trust God regardless of what you may face in all areas of your life? If not, what's stopping you from trusting God completely?

Are there areas of your life you have not completely surrendered to God?

How do you respond to the following? "The way you go about your testing is your choice. It is the attitude of your heart."

What experiences have you had with others that involve trust? Did you move on after the trust was broken?

If not, what kept you from trusting that person or persons again?

Can you bring the matter to God now?

Have you ever not been able to forgive someone?

What was the effect that had on you?

How could you benefit by forgiving others and maybe yourself?

Is there someone or something you need to forgive or receive forgiveness for? Bring it to God.

What are you fearful of?

Are there valid reasons for your fear?

How can you be free from your fears?

Are you at the right place in regard to your relationship with God? If not, what needs to change?

Is there an area in your life that is not pleasing to God? Obedience, sin, etc.?

Does this behavior affect others?

What steps can you take to stop this behavior?

Chapter 12
Love

You must love the lord your God with all your heart, all your soul, all your mind and your strength. The second

is equally important: Love your neighbor as yourself.
No other commandment is greater than these.
—Mark 12:30

How are you doing in the areas of

- loving God:
- loving self:
- loving others:

What areas are you struggling with? Why is that?

Do you want to grow in these areas? Ask God now to increase and grow love in your heart in these areas.

Read 1 Corinthians 13 again. What are your thoughts?

Chapter 13
Living the Abundant Life

The thief comes only to steal and kill and destroy; I have
come that they may have life, and have it to the full.
—John 10:10 NIV

How do you interpret this verse?

On what side of the coma do you currently live—the last part after the coma, or before the coma?

What are the benefits of living before the coma?

What are the benefits of living after the coma?

Can you break with the wrong beliefs and habits of the past?

No dear brothers and sister, I have not achieved it, but I focus on this one thing: Forgetting the past and looking forward to what lies ahead, I press on to reach the end of the race and receive the heavenly prize for which God, through Christ Jesus, is calling us.
—Philippians 3:13–14

Have you been able to embrace new beliefs, truths, and habits?

Have you experienced any results yet? What are they?

Can you embrace your identity in Christ Jesus?

Have you found a key verse that you have made your own? Write it out here.

And now, dear brothers and sisters, one final thing. Fix your thoughts on what is true and honorable, and right, and pure, and lovely, and admirable. Think about things that are excellent and worthy of praise. Keep putting into practice all you learned and received from me – everything you heard from and saw me doing. Then the God of peace will be with you.
—Philippians 4:8

I pray you will grow in your identity in Christ Jesus and know God loves you. I pray he will guide you every step of the way. I pray you will lean on Him and trust him with all your needs, pains, disappointments, and uncertainty. I pray that as you are on your journey, weariness and hopelessness will not overtake you. I pray your eyes will stay focused on Him, the author and finisher of your faith. I pray you will grow in your love for Him and for others each new day. I pray you will grow in your knowledge and understanding of our great and awesome God. I pray you will walk in the confidence that our God can bring about everything you ask for.

All glory to God, who is able through his mighty power at work in us to accomplish infinitely more than we might ask or think (Ephesians 3:20).

Printed in the United States
By Bookmasters